Necessary Ingredients for a Simple Existence: The Transformation

A N.I.S.E. Book

Maria C. Pimentel-Gannon

Copyright © 2015 by Maria C. Pimentel-Gannon

All rights reserved.

Book design by Maria C. Pimentel-Gannon

No part of this book may be reproduced in any form or by any electronic or mechanical means, including information storage and retrieval systems, without permission in writing from the author. The only exception is by a reviewer, who may quote short excerpts in a review.

Available for order through Ingram Press Catalogues

Maria C. Pimentel-Gannon
Visit my website at www.asimpleexistence.com

Printed in the United States of America
First Printing: April 2016
Published by Sojourn Publishing, LLC

ISBN: 978-1-62747-114-5
Ebook ISBN: 978-1-62747-115-2

DEDICATION

This book is for those who have seen the amazing power of the illogical and for those who long to see it. This book is for those who are ready to believe and ready to hope - - - for those who are ready to acknowledge the power of the extraordinary in the life of the ordinary. This book is dedicated to those who will open themselves to finding inspiration and hope, happiness and joy, faith and trust, and most of all, encouragement, in the pages of this book.

I dedicate this NISE book, and all future NISE books, to God, through whom ALL things are possible.

I dedicate this book to my amazing family: my husband, Jack; my daughter, Jacqueline; my daughter, Veronica, and her husband, Peter Seroter; and my wonderful ninety-one year old mother, Irene Pimentel. I dedicate it to them because of who they are in my life, but also because of all they did to support and contribute to the publication of this book.

I dedicate this book to those who helped me above and beyond the call of duty: Jack, Henry, Karyl, Gene, Vince, Robyn, and Lydia.

I dedicate this book to my surrogate daughter, Renee, whose life ended unexpectedly and too soon at the age of 28. She and her parents, Karyl and Gene, have been loyal and wonderful throughout our many years of friendship.

I also dedicate this book to the deceased members of my family and very close friends, whose lives I want to acknowledge through the writing of this first book: Lorraine P, Yolanda O, Angie B, Rafael R, Fernando D, Freddie D, Teddy B, Olga B, John and Marie G, Colleen G, Kevin K, and Jack H.

INTRODUCTION

Thank you, sincerely, for reading this introduction. I hope that in it you will read something that interests you and excites you to read the book. I wish there were some way that I could tell you everything I want you to know about this book, but it's just not possible in a brief introduction. This book was written for whomever will receive its message.

In editing the book, I had to read it several times. I must confess that each time I read it, I enjoyed the book more and more. At the risk of sounding vain, I have to tell you that with each read, I laughed and I cried. It truly is a good read – not because I wrote it, but because it was divinely inspired – and it is a quick read! It is a good read filled with hope and with lessons on how we might discover God in the daily and ordinary, recognize Him, acknowledge His presence, fall in love with Him, and lead a spiritually simple existence. I thoroughly enjoy the book, and I hope you will, too.

This book is about "Necessary Ingredients for a Simple Existence" a.k.a., N.I.S.E. or NISE. It is a story about a part of my life that is full of passion . . . full of awe . . . full of love. These things are what I want to share with each one of you. In these pages, you will find something that is very personal, but personal in a different way. It happened to me, but hopefully, you can personalize it to your own life. It is about living life simply so that you can simply live.

Perhaps I can better tell you what this book is not. It is not a book that was written by an expert at anything. It is not intending to prove the existence of God based on science and research, nor is it a book promising to provide a "quick fix" to life's struggles and heartaches. In fact, it would be a disservice to any fellow human being to offer a way OUT of pain and suffering, because it is THROUGH pain and suffering that we are refined and molded to fully become the person each of us is created to be.

This is the story of how I once was blind, but now I see. It sounds like a cliché, but it is true. I knew of God, but I did not personally know him, nor did I understand Him or what He was truly about. God had been revealing himself to me all my life, yet it was only a little more than thirty-three years ago that I was able to "see" Him, recognize Him, experience Him, and acknowledge Him. Once I was able to see and recognize God in my life, our eyes locked and have remained that way ever since.

This is the journey of how God manifested Himself to me in ways that are truly amazing. He started teaching me to live and not just exist . . . to thrive and not just to live . . . and to be not just to do . . . and to do it all simply. He taught me that less is more and that simplicity begets abundance.

He taught me that life is sometimes not easy, but it can be simple. *And* He proved to me just how *REAL* He ***truly*** is.

What if, for just one day, no matter the circumstances of the day, you were content and experienced true joy? What if you learned how to live this way permanently? There can be nothing more empowering than being able to exercise power over any situation, no matter how difficult or ugly the situation. *This* type of life leads to fulfillment. It draws power, to some degree from within, but *mostly from above*.

The second most translated book in the world after the Bible is *Purpose Driven Life* by Pastor Rick Warren. The first line of this life-changing book is, "It's not about you." While this statement is countercultural, I could not agree more. I have learned this truth – life is *NOT* about me. It is about *God* and about God's love for me and for all humanity. My story, the story of how I went from living to thriving, of how I once was blind, but now I see, is not about me. It is about how God will use my experiences for His greater purpose.

Indeed, it is not about me. Nevertheless, it *is* about my sharing with you some of my "God-moments" or "divine appointments" … powerful moments that forever changed my life.

Have you ever seen something unfold right before your very eyes that simply defied logic? You try to wrap your head around it, but you are simply left speechless and in awe. In this book, you will read about instances where things like this happened. I usually am not one to use words that are clichés; consequently, I reserve the use of the word "awesome" to times that are truly amazing! I can tell you that the experiences you will read about in this book show the awesomeness of God – awesomeness that defies logic – in the life of a person who is simple in her lifestyle and simple in her living.

In a world that values self and "stuff," simplicity can be found. We have become a society that is all about "MORE" and "NOW" as a desperate attempt towards happiness and fulfillment. The more we add materialism and negativity to our life, the more our life (that was intended to be beautiful) becomes complicated.

My hope is that you will love this book as much as I loved writing it and sharing my story – God's story – with you. My prayer is that no matter your religious, cultural, or educational background, no matter your gender, age, or race, you will feel encouraged and inspired to "Let go, and let God" so that you might gain a new, better, and more simple existence. That would be so "nice."

Peace be with you.
Maria Pimentel-Gannon, A.F.T.L.
(Ambassador For The Lord)

NECESSARY INGREDIENTS FOR A SIMPLE EXISTENCE:
The Transformation

It was many years ago – I remember the day vividly – the day my life changed. I did not know then that my life would be changing; I only knew what I was feeling at the moment. I remember that day as if it were yesterday. The road was ahead of me. I was driving. The rain came down, and with the rain came my tears. As I drove on that interstate, I talked with God. I pleaded with Him. I asked Him question after question. "What do You *want* from me?" "What is Your *purpose* for me?"

I was at a crossroads in my life. I had just taken a big leap of faith. I had done something – something that would forever change my life. I, who had been working since a very young age, had promised the Lord that I would stop working full-time to become primarily a stay-at-home mom and housewife. Both titles seemed so very foreign to me. But a promise is a promise – especially to God.

As the tears slid down my cheeks and my face, I wiped them away with the back of my hand to the time of the windshield wipers' gentle rhythm. Through glistening eyes, I made my way to my destination.

Even as a child, all I ever wanted to do in my life was to please God and to live my life according to the plan and the purpose He had for me. But I did not know what that plan or purpose was. All I wanted from Him was to let me know His plan and purpose for me. All I wanted was for Him to reveal it to me somehow. I wanted to know why I was here in the world. I wanted to know my purpose in life. I wanted to know what life was all about. Whatever the purpose, I just wanted to know it so that I could fulfill it.

At one time in my life, I wanted to change the world. I wanted to help bring about world peace. I wanted to make a big and positive difference in the world back then, and I still do, but perhaps not as naïvely or idealistically. I did not know what that would or could look like, so I asked. That was what opened the floodgates to my tears on that special, memorable, and life-changing day that would be one of several to come.

I knew that I wanted to live my life for God, but I did not really *know* God – not on a personal level. It was a head knowledge and not so much a heart knowledge that I had of God up to that point. Now, all I could do was to weep and ache – not a painful ache, but a yearning, an ache of wanting to do something profound in order to be able to fulfill my calling, and an ache of not knowing what to do. I did not want to disappoint the only Father I had ever really known.

Therefore, I asked God again what He wanted from me. I asked how I could serve Him, especially now that my whole life was changing. He had been silent for a long time, and I had not been able to hear His voice through the years. I understand now that it had not been my time to have this knowledge revealed; more importantly, it had not yet been ***His*** time. Suddenly, on that drive, I heard something. As I drove in the rain that fateful day, my heavenly Father was giving me something. He was talking to me, but I did not understand. I asked for clarity, but He just kept giving me the same thing. I kept hearing it over and over. "Nice." "Nice." "Nice." With a feeling of bewilderment I asked, "Nice? What does that mean?" Then He poured the words profusely into my mind, into my head, and more importantly, into my heart and my soul. He allowed me to begin to see the image of the plans He had for me.

It was then that I knew. I knew what God was saying to me. I knew...because I knew...because I knew...that He was saying N – I – S – E, NISE: Necessary Ingredients for a Simple Existence. He was not saying "nice" – He was saying "NISE".

He wanted me to finally begin to write – to write "His" stories. He had let me know so many years ago that I was to write. I knew it all along, even as a young girl. I wanted to do it, but through the years, I kept putting it off. I simply let life happen, and I let life take control of me rather than allowing God, or even myself, to take control of my life. I let the opportunities to write pass me by. And He was calling me to begin to fulfill my life's purpose. He wanted me to stop letting the opportunities to fulfill that purpose keep passing me by. He wanted me to do it **NOW**. He wanted me to convey to others that He wants us to "live simply, so that we may simply live" . . . in Him. And He wanted me to do it through my writing. But what did He mean by that? What did it mean to "live simply, so that we may simply live?"

He answered me right away. God was giving me the "necessary ingredients" to obey His will for my life, to do His work. Suddenly, it gushed out. I knew. Yes, I knew. He wanted me to write a series of "NISE" books, probably little in size, but with "nice," big, and powerful messages. I was to write a series of books, most of which would contain stories – stories of love . . . of faith . . . of miracles; stories of hope and forgiveness and redemption. Stories that so visibly and powerfully show the presence of God, that show the power of His love, as well as His mercy, His grace, His forgiveness, and His faithfulness; stories through which anyone could be awed and touched by how God works.

I started hearing Him faster than I could think. The downpour of my tears cleared my eyes. I was able to see clearly what it was that He was saying. He wanted me to write; not just a book, but BOOKS. For this purpose, ALL of them would be "NISE" books. I grabbed a pen and paper and started writing down these thoughts as I drove, especially the titles He was giving me. Suddenly it all made sense. He was saying lots of things: Necessary Ingredients for Spiritual Enlightenment, Necessary Ingredients for Spiritual Existence . . . for Spiritual Enhancement . . . for Successful Existence . . . for Social Etiquette . . . for Spanish Enrichment . . . for Spanish Enhancement . . . for Social Engagement . . . for Social Enrichment . . . for Spiritual Engagement . . . for Special Evangelization . . . for Spiritual Evangelization . . . for Self Expression . . . for Self Evaluation . . . for Special Education . . . Necessary Ingredients for so many things. The possibilities seemed endless.

I was so excited. I was elated. My mind was ablaze and my heart was racing. I could barely contain my excitement and enthusiasm. Now I had new tears – tears of realization and enlightenment; tears of gratitude and joy and relief. Mine were now tears brought on by undeserved grace. I was so grateful to the Lord for having shown me His will for the direction of my life, for having shown me His plans for me. "For I know the plans I have for you," says the Lord. (Jeremiah 29:11) This was the segue for me to share "His-story" with others, as well as my own history. But, when was this to happen? *How* was this to begin?

That day He inspired me to go to the next level – to go deeper within. And I did. Regrettably, it would be years before I would do something serious with what He had given me ... before I would write about the beauty and awe in this life, in this world – about ***HIS*** beauty and ***HIS*** awesomeness. In the process, God helped me to understand that even though I feel that I failed in not writing this series of books any sooner, in the end, it is ALL God's timing. And God's timing is perfect, and there is a time and purpose and a season for everything under Heaven. (Ecclesiastes 3:1-8) In life, we, as humans, make mistakes, but God does not!

Yes, God was calling me to write books. At the same time, He was calling me to do something more. He was calling me not just to write about it, but also to live it. He wanted me to live out my own spiritual journey. He wanted me to *live* nice and simple ingredients for a simple existence so that I could **write** about them, so that I could write about NISE.

It would not be until editing this book that the realization hit me that I could not have started writing God's stories about everything that I've mentioned thus far – about living in and experiencing that deep, unconditional, and abiding love with God, about having a personal relationship with Jesus Christ, about being born again – until I had had these experiences myself. In order for these stories to be authentic and transparent, God had a work to do in me. I had to go through my own journey of spiritual and personal transformation. I began that life-long journey in 1982 and now, at last, God was ready for me to write.

2

God wanted me to share with people that He is everywhere. That He is in the ordinary – often times in extraordinary ways. All we need to do is to recognize Him and to acknowledge Him. God wants us to be open to the possibility and the reality that He **DOES** exist and that He **IS** for real. He wants us to make ourselves *accessible* to Him, to open ourselves to Him so that we can *see* Him, *recognize* Him, AND *acknowledge* Him. He wants me to remind people of this. He wants me to use real-life, firsthand experiences to convey that He is, indeed, for real. He wants people to know that He *knows each* of us individually and that we are not only real to Him, but He also **REALLY** knows us each by name, and He *truly* knows every strand of hair on each of our heads. He wants His stories to speak of His faithfulness and His sovereignty. He wants me to speak of His realness, not just for me, but also for YOU and for ALL. Mostly, God wants me to let others know, through these NISE little books, of the great, immense love He has for each one of us. It took years for me to realize to what God was calling me and to discern how this was meant to come about. However, I knew that God had prepared me for this time and season of my life. "For God has prepared you for such a time as this." (Esther 4:14)

Through this discovery process, this process of enlightenment and writing, He also revealed other things to me. He revealed to me that I had to personally learn and to grow before He could use me to impact the lives of others. After all, one's credibility comes from one's experiences in life and how one handles those experiences. Therefore, I could not have started writing before now because I had not yet experienced simple and successful existence, that is, until now.

Prior to this revelation, all I could think about was how I had failed to obey God's calling to write. Through the years, I had tried preparing for, and had given thought to, this purpose that God had intended for me. I had created letterhead stationery for my NISE endeavors and then waited. I got business cards with the NISE name on it. I waited to see what God was going to do with it.

Even without knowing its ultimate significance or purpose, NISE has been a part of my life in some way or another through the years. At meetings, I would introduce myself and when asked "who" I was with, I would say I was with NISE. I did consulting, so when asked what I did, I would say that I was a NISE Consultant. Of course, people heard "nice" consultant. No doubt, some of them thought I was saying that I was "nice." They did not know what I was talking about, so I am certain that some of them thought I was bragging or that it was my "catch" phrase. Those who were interested, asked me; those who weren't, made assumptions or simply seemed not to care. Yes, through the years, God had allowed me to do different things with NISE, but His time had not yet come for me to write His NISE books.

3

Initially, I could not begin to fathom the depth of God's purpose; I could not process it. I did not fully understand it. I knew something was happening, but I did not know what it was, so I kept on with the routine of my life. Now I understand. Now I know. Now I am ready for anyone and everyone who may read this book, or any one of the other books to come, to get an understanding of *WHO* God is, to get a glimpse of His love and to get a firsthand view of His divine manifestation.

The years went by, and I continued doing what I had been doing with NISE – very little. Or so I thought. God was preparing me. He had to meld me, to mold me, and to fill me, so He could use me. I was not ready back then to be entrusted with such an amazing privilege. Therefore, He had me go through my own "simple" experiences. The first of these experiences was the pinnacle of my life. It is the story of my conversion. I share this story later in the book. The second of these experiences was when God gave me the revelation about NISE.

Another of these experiences was in the spring of 1983. For the first time in my life, I went on a retreat. More than a retreat, it was a spiritual encounter. It was a life experience – one of renewal. Back then, I didn't even know what renewal was, let alone know what I was renewing. I was entering into a world that was completely new to me. Up to then, my spiritual world was private, and it was minimal. I went to church. I did the Sunday thing. I was what I now call a "pew/bench warmer." There was nothing really "wrong" with that. I did the right thing, the obligatory thing, but I was not invested in or committed to what I was doing. And I did it for the wrong reasons. I went to church, and I prayed while I was at church. I prayed outside of church, but that, too, was rote and routine.

This "praying," or this "pew-warming" way of going to church, is not to be confused with faith. I've always been a person of great faith. Back then, it was a faith that came from my upbringing. It came from what I had learned, from what I had been taught. I lived a "simple" faith of a different kind (because I did not have personal, firsthand knowledge or experience of God), as opposed to living my faith simply, as I do now. Now, my faith defines me, as does my love for God.

I had been a person who would go to church, and if I arrived late, I did not feel guilty because after all, I was taking time from my schedule to fulfill this obligation. Whether I arrived late, early, or on time, the end was still usually the same – I would leave as early and as quickly as possible. I would rush out to try and beat the people traffic and then the car traffic. I did not know people around me, so it was easy to do. And I did not make it a point to get to know people or even to meet them. I was merely in church with other people doing *their* Sunday duty.

When I went to this weekend experience of renewal, something awakened in me. I did not know it at the time. I only knew that something had happened and that something was different. On this weekend experience I had done things and experienced feelings that I had never experienced before. I know now that it was my "spiritual awakening." I know now that God had whispered in my ear, just like He had whispered in my ear about NISE. However, this time, I was listening . . . and I could hear . . . and I was ready.

4

What I know today is different from what I knew then. As I mentioned previously, it was in 1982 that I had my powerful, personal, and spiritual conversion. I will share more about this conversion with you later in the book.

It was shortly after that experience of conversion that God would enlighten me about NISE. Then it was March of 1983 that I would go on the spiritual weekend of renewal. That weekend was called Christ Renews His Parish, but for me, it was called Christ Renews His People, and in my case, His child. That is what He had done for me; He had called me, and He had renewed me . . . His child.

However, the painful truth that I will share with you is that He had called me and that I had answered, but *only* because it served my purpose, my personal plans at that time. At least that is what I thought then. What God knew, and what I would later discover, is that it was the eve of my spiritual enlightenment. I went on that "retreat" only because I was pregnant. As I mentioned previously, in actuality, it is *not* a retreat; it is a life-changing, life-transforming

experience. It is the beginning of a process and of a spiritual journey ... and this is exactly what happened, and continues to happen, to me.

I was new in town, and I needed and wanted to find a church that I could attend so that I could meet people. And I was in a hurry to do so. I needed to meet people because I wanted to have a baby shower (more on this later). I wanted to give birth to my new baby, my miracle baby, but not alone. I had no one around me because I knew no one around me. I wanted to meet people so that I would have someone to visit me while in the hospital. I had no family in town, and neither did my husband. I came from a big family, and so did he; yet we were all alone in this city, and we had no close "friends." He had acquaintances at work; I had left behind all my friends and acquaintances in the little town where we had lived and from where we had moved.

I had to hurry, I had to allow time to get to know others so that they would feel that they wanted to throw a baby shower for me. So after "church shopping" for a while, perhaps a few months, we came back to this one church that was racially and socio-economically more diverse than the others we visited. It was not a very big church at the time, but it was a church.

N.I.S.E.: The Transformation

Then I saw it. I was reading their bulletin and I happened upon a little blurb – "Are you new to the parish?" Yes. "Do you want to meet people?" Yes. "Would you like to meet other women and possibly have new friendships?" Yes. "Do you want to pray with other women?" Not particularly; but if that's what it takes. "Do you want to take some time out of your busy schedule to just stop and listen to God and to pray?" Not necessarily, but if that's what it takes. "Then come to this weekend." Okay. "Come to refresh and renew" is what I now know God was telling me. If these were the things I had to do to have a baby shower thrown for me, then I would do them.

Something that I have learned in life is that God has such a sense of humor, and many times He shows it just to illustrate to us how ridiculous and impractical we are sometimes being in our requests or prayers. In reality, His sense of humor is so that we can learn . . . not to be taught a lesson, but rather, to *learn* a lesson, a life skill, something that will benefit us and perhaps others. God's sense of humor also keeps us humble. I have always felt, and sometimes said, that a good student will learn everything they can, as much as they can, whenever they can, wherever they can, and that the world is their classroom and life is their teacher. Personally, I try to be a good student of life, and I can assure you that I have learned so incredibly much and that God has taught me much humility!

Yes, God brought me on this weekend to this group of women to get what I wanted. I would later learn that the weekends usually drew large groups of women – around 25 people attending and 25 hosting the weekend. Lots of potential for a baby shower, maybe even multiple showers. (Oh me, of weak and self-serving faith!) My group had twelve women, myself included. In time, it would dwindle to ten, and eventually eight. Nonetheless, this small group of women gave me what I wanted. They gave me a shower, and for that, I was grateful.

Yes, this small group of women had been kind enough to give me what had been my heart's desire at the time: to have a shower for my unborn baby. The baby that was my miracle. The baby that was an answer to prayer. The baby that God had allowed me to conceive against all odds. The baby that God had used to turn me and my life around, so that I would be open to His plan for me and to be fertile soil for Him to plant His seeds. Seeds that would through the years produce abundantly. Seeds that would yield what God wanted. How did I get so lucky – forgive me, luck has nothing to do with this. How, and why, did I get so blessed? Who would have known that the experience of having this baby would do so much to teach me, that this experience would be the cause of turning my life around? I just thank God that He caught my attention. I thank God that He was patient with me, that He took the time with me, and that He did with me what He did, because in 1982, and then again in 1983, God got ahold of me – and He has not let go since.

5

The way God got ahold of me was the turning point of my life. It was my epiphany, my revelation; it was my God-moment. In 1982 I experienced my divine appointment, my wow-moment, my life-changing manifestation ... and my conversion!

Before getting married, I had gynecological surgery. I married my best friend the year after my first surgery. Soon after that, I had more health issues. I was told that in all probability I would not be able to conceive. At the time I heard this news, it did not seem too consequential. I was working, I had a good job, and that was what was important. My husband loved me and supported me, so if I were okay with not having children, he would be, too. Or so we thought.

As can be imagined, I started seeing babies everywhere, seeing women who were pregnant and who seemed very happy being pregnant. I saw women with children, and I saw so many families around. They laughed. They played. They would even smile at me. I started to yearn for what I could not have. I started to get an ache in my heart, a fluttering of my soul, that I would never be that picture – of a mom with her child, nor of a mom and dad with children ... of FAMILY. I started longing for children. My husband saw that longing, but there was nothing we could do about it, other than to have fun trying.

I had heard that one could talk to God and that He would listen. So I started "talking" to Him – I now know that I was praying. I did not know then that praying was just talking to God. I was letting Him know what I wanted; it never crossed my mind to ask Him what *He* wanted for me. Then I started to barter with Him. Clearly, He had not understood what I had been asking of Him, so I began to try to find ways for Him to hear me and to grant me my request.

I did not have much to barter nor much to offer, and even if I did, I had no idea what I should be bartering, so I offered a thing that would not be much of a sacrifice, but sounded sacrificial. This way, it would not be too hard to make the "sacrifice" and to keep my word, should God decide to grant me my request. I told God that if He let me get pregnant and have a child, I would give up drinking. Of course, I knew that this was no big deal for me because I was not much of a drinker. I knew that *He* knew that, but perhaps it was something He could and would overlook. Nothing happened.

Then I thought about what else I could use as a bartering tool. I thought of smoking. I would give up smoking. *This* would have been a major sacrifice. At the time, I thought I enjoyed smoking. I smoked a good bit. Actually, I did not fully smoke the cigarettes; mostly, they burned in the ashtray. I had an office job, and the cigarettes burned while I worked at my desk. Every once in a while I would get a good inhale. And I certainly enjoyed a cigarette during special times: with a cup of coffee, when drinking socially, and after wonderful, intimate times with my husband.

Even though smoking was not a healthy thing to do, giving it up would be a sacrifice. It would be hard to give up, not just physically, but mentally and emotionally. Weirdly enough, I enjoyed puffing on the cigarettes, gently inhaling and slowly exhaling the smoke. I liked having the cigarette between my fingers, raising the cigarette up to my lips, puffing, and then watching the smoke make little circles above me. I actually enjoyed smoking, so it was indeed a sacrifice for me to give it up. I was giving God one of my best bartering chips. He had to know just how big this sacrifice was for me, because after all, He knew everything – didn't He? However, it was a sacrifice

I was willing to make for the sake of having a baby. Still, nothing happened.

When God still did not grant me the desire of my heart, I started to wonder why. I started spending more time talking to God. I tried to listen, though I must confess that back then, I did not really know how to "hear" God or how to discern His voice. Nonetheless, I found myself spending more time in quiet moments. More time "being still." Trying to follow God's instruction to "Be still and know that I am God." (Psalm 46:10) And this time, I was not as blasé as I had been in my request. This time I asked Him from the heart . . . and I spoke to Him most lovingly from deep within my heart. "Am I really not supposed to have a baby? Am I really to go through life without knowing what it is to bear a child, to experience motherhood – to experience the miracle of life, to experience giving birth to my child, whose beautiful tiny body would be held in my arms? Am I not to experience the love being transmitted into my baby the moment he or she suckles at my breast? Am I to be denied the unbelievable and miraculous privilege and opportunity to know that I would be leaving my legacy behind through my child?" I did not know, but I hoped not.

I continued to talk to God, but I started talking to Him on a more personal and intimate level. I truly and sincerely wanted to know. I asked if there were anything in the world, anything from my meager possessions, that I could offer Him in exchange for a child. This time He answered me. He let me know. He wanted me to give up my "little god."

"Little god," I questioned? What was that? I had never heard of that before. I did not have a little god. If I did, what was it?

Up to that point, I had lived and breathed for my job. I loved it. I worked with a wonderful population. I was working for the State of Indiana, and I worked specifically with the program that served seasonal and migrant farm workers. They were a good, hard-working, and long-suffering people. I was working for a state agency that could help them. I had started my work with this segment of the population as a Counselor, but had moved up to the position of Regional Director, the leader, the one with whom the buck stopped.

The staff and I were trying to help this population enter into the mainstream. Ours was a program that helped those who chose to leave the migrant and farm labor lifestyle. We offered them the opportunity to learn English, to go to school, or to learn a new vocation. Whatever their desire was, we would help and support them in it. Whatever the need, we would try to help them meet it. We would help pay their schooling or help them while training on the job. We would help them find housing, and if necessary, help them with their rent until they could get on their feet.

I was doing something with a purpose. I felt like I was making a difference in the lives of these people. It felt good to make a difference in someone's life. I felt that I made a big difference in my little world. I loved my job, but mostly, I loved the people that I had the opportunity to serve. I felt needed. So when God told me that my *job* was my "little god," I felt puzzled. I did not know what He meant. I did not understand, nor could I comprehend, what He was trying to tell me. I had thought all along that I was doing a good thing, that I was helping people in need, and therefore, that I was pleasing *Him*.

I asked Him what He meant by "little god." He gently and lovingly let me know that I let my job come before everything and everyone else – including my husband and even myself, but especially before Him. He helped me to see that I did not think twice about missing church services, if it meant helping our clients. Many of them had become close acquaintances, almost friends. I loved them, and I felt they loved me. I felt that they needed me, and I felt good being needed. I loved serving them so much that serving them, and especially feeling needed, indeed had become my "little god." In addition, God showed me that I was a workaholic. Serving and helping others was so important to me that it became a vice. I needed it. I probably needed it more than the people I served needed me. Therefore, I worked endlessly and tirelessly.

So I asked God, "Are You saying that if I am willing to give up my job, You will let me have a child?" I cannot say that I heard an audible voice saying "YES," but I knew in the heart of my heart, that that was precisely what God was asking of me. So I thought about it, and I pondered my answer. Would I? Could I? Not surprisingly, I started seeing even more and more babies and moms with their babies, and more families together – laughing, living life abundantly.

Suddenly, it hit me. Yes, I would do it. Of course I would! I would give up my job. I told God that if He would give me a baby, I would give Him my job, and I would let go of my "little god." And I would be faithful to Him, my *true* God.

In spite of this insight, I have to confess and to be honest. Even though I knew God could do ***anything*** He wanted to do, and that He could perform ***any*** miracle He wanted to perform, I was not sure that He would give me what I wanted.

Nonetheless, I thought I would test the waters by being willing to give up my "little god."

Time went on, and the desire to have a baby grew, but I no longer made the request the same way I had made it initially. This time, when I prayed about it, I did so with sincere humility and earnestness. I put it in His hands . . . this time with a sincere faith. I told Him that if it were His will, I would accept a child, and that I would try to raise the child to the best of my ability. I told Him that I would try to be aware of all my actions from that point on to avoid creating other little gods. I told Him that if He wanted, I would give up my full-time job and that I would only work part-time thereafter. I would make myself fully available to Him. I would serve *Him*, and *only* Him, and when serving others, I would do so in *His* name, not my own, to *His* glory, and not my own. I would allow Him to use me in whatever way He willed. I told God that I would be His *fully*, and that I would offer my child, my husband, my marriage, my family, and my **all** to Him – for *His* glory and for *His* praise.

During one of my many conversations with God when I pleaded with Him to let me have a child, He questioned me as to who would raise my child. He let me see that I was asking so badly for a child, but I had not stopped to consider the responsibilities and all the other things that having a child entails. After all, who *would* take care of my child? I had no family in town. If I were so busy with my job and my volunteer and ministry work and had such little time left for my husband, my home, and even myself, how could I ever have time to take care of my own child? God had certainly given me a lot to think about. He *made* me think. He caused me to reflect. He caused me to look deep down inside myself and to ponder things that I had never before contemplated.

My husband loved me a lot (and he still does), and I loved him (and still do). We were always together. At the end of his work day, he would come to my office. At the time, he was the manager of the local office of a state agency. He would often bring dinner for us, and we would eat there in my office. Many times, he would help me with some of the managerial paper work. As Regional Director of our Center, I was now in charge of the whole office. There were four offices in the state. Mine was the largest office, had the most staff and the largest budget. It covered and served the greatest number of counties and had the largest client base. A state car was assigned to each office, and specifically to the Regional Directors. By worldly standards, I had a wonderful and prestigious job, and I felt like I was on top of the world.

6

Time marched on. I continued to desire to have a baby. I continued to work, and I continued to be a workaholic. After all, God had not yet granted me the desire of my heart. I had not considered at that time that it *could* have been possible that God would not allow me to get pregnant. I had not considered that He might have had a different and broader plan for me and have had a reason for me to not have a child. All I knew was that God was all- powerful and that He could do whatever He wanted. I never considered the possibility that my husband and I might truly be childless. I was so naïve!

Then I came down with a serious case of pneumonia. I had been through two rounds of antibiotics for the pneumonia; I now needed a third. My husband always accompanied me to my doctor appointments, and I accompanied him to his (although he is the epitome of good health, thanks be to God, and he seldom sees the doctor). As the office manager, he could take the time, when needed, to go with me. We did everything together. But when it was time to go see the doctor to get my new antibiotic, I told him not to bother to come. I did not want him to waste his time. He insisted on coming, and I insisted that I did not want to take him from his job to accompany me just to pick up some antibiotics. He finally agreed to not come along.

I sat in the doctor's office on the examination table, being examined by a doctor who was filling in for my regular doctor, chatting with him and answering his questions while he looked at my medical records. Suddenly his next question was, "So, how long have you been pregnant?" My legs had been swinging back and forth as I sat there. The swing never skipped a beat as I told him, "Oh, I'm not pregnant. I'm just here for more medicine for this persistent pneumonia." He looked at me, looked back at whatever he had been looking at, and said, "You *are* pregnant," to which I answered, "No, I'm not. I'm not sure what you are looking at, but you have the wrong person."

To this date, I cannot recall on what he based that declaration, but in writing this book I got to thinking that I must have given him a urine specimen. It's funny how I had not remembered that detail until writing about this experience. All these years I had wondered how he had known I was pregnant! His response to me was, "Well, I don't know, but this rabbit died," an expression that was used in those days when a pregnancy test came back positive. Suddenly, my legs stopped swinging. I sat up straighter, and I asked him if he could repeat what he had just said. He told me, "You are pregnant. How long have you been pregnant?"

Suddenly, I could no longer hear what he was saying. My head started to spin, and things got fuzzy. Thoughts ran quickly through my mind. The very first thing I thought of was that I had denied my husband the opportunity to hear what we both had longed to hear for some time. And *suddenly,* all I could think of was about what I had promised God – those bargaining chips. Let me see. Okay, I could stop drinking; I don't want to hurt the baby. Smoking? That was going to take some time, and yes, it would be difficult, but I could do it. I would stop smoking. Immediately. I didn't want to hurt the baby. What else? Let me think. My job!?! Oh my gosh, my job!

Instantly, I thought about all the people I was serving at the time. Their faces ran before my eyes – the smiling faces, the tears, the laughter, the wrinkles on the tanned faces, the scratches on the hands. Their skin that was dark and tanned and tough from the sun, the wind, the rain, and other elements of nature. Before me, I saw their eyes with looks of pain, of wonder, of sadness, of hope, of gratitude, and of a multitude of feelings known only to each individually. How was I going to walk away from all of that? How was I going to turn my back on any one of them? What about Roberto? Or Yolanda? Or Juanita? Or Jesús (also known as 'Chuey')? Or any one of the many who I had grown to love? Could I do it?

Yes, I could. But how? How was I going to say goodbye to each one of them, and greater yet, how was I going to be able to keep my promise to God? How were we going to manage without the additional household income? ***How***?!?

First, and more importantly, how was I going to share this wonderful news with my husband, and how was I going to apologize to him for having talked him into not coming with me? Oh, he would forgive me; he knew it was not deliberate. He would be sorrier for me that he had not been there. He knew how much I would have wanted him with me to receive the good news. But still, I felt badly that he had not been with me to hear the wonderful news!

I don't remember what all happened after that. I walked away in a dream-like state, trying to process what I had just been told and what that meant for me now. NEVER, EVER would my life be the same again . . . EVER . . . for **many** reasons and at many levels.

Somehow, at some point, I shared the good news with my husband. To this day, I cannot recall how or when that happened (I feel better that neither can he). Our joy could not be contained! I think he was happier for me because I was so incredibly happy. He wanted my happiness more than anything.

Then came the hard part: my JOB! I needed to leave my job, to walk away from it. To prepare for a new way of living, a new lifestyle, and a new life – both the baby's and mine. Our little family would soon be three. I immediately stopped drinking, which you might recall I did not do much of anyway. The smoking was tougher than I had realized it would be. I realized that my body was addicted to the nicotine, just like my emotions, my mind, my head, and my spirit had been addicted to feeling needed and to serving others. I realized that at some point, I had gotten out of balance with my being. But for now, my focus was that, if God had kept His word and His end of the bargain, then I would have to keep mine.

I stopped smoking cold turkey. I did not even take that one last cigarette. I did not give the pack away. I did not want to do that. I knew that smoking was not good for my health; I certainly did not want to give the cancer sticks to anyone else. As frugal as I was (and still am) and as much as I did not (and still don't) like to waste, I threw that expensive pack of cigarettes away. And it was almost a full pack! That handsome, rugged Marlboro Man and I were through.

7

Now came the part that I dreaded – walking away from my job. I shared my angst with my husband. I opened my heart and soul to him. I exposed my deepest feelings and rawest emotions to him. I tried to explain why it was so difficult for me to give up my job – the people I would be saying goodbye to, the prestige, etc. His response surprised me, and it certainly blindsided me! He could not understand why I was feeling so much angst. He said that the solution was easy. I asked him how he could think it was easy. He said, "You just ***don't*** stop working."

"And how am I going to do that?" I asked. "After all, I made a promise, and a promise is a promise, especially to God!"

"Oh, come on, Mari," (his endearing name for me) "you don't really think that God is going to hold you to that promise, do you?"

I could not believe my ears. Were those words really coming out of my husband's mouth? Was I really hearing what I was actually hearing, or were my head and ears playing games with me? I could not wrap my head around the fact that he seemed to be unaware of and oblivious to my feelings and emotions.

"What do you mean, Jack?"

"You don't think God took you seriously, or that He is going to hold you to your word, do you?" Still incredulous, but now mixed with shock, hurt, disappointment, and even anger, I said, "Why *wouldn't* He? I made a promise. I took *Him* seriously, and I took him at *His* word. Why wouldn't He take me at *mine?* You know how I feel about a promise. I hardly *ever* make a promise. When I *do* make a promise, I do EVERYTHING within my power to keep that promise. You know how I am about my word. Just like when we got married. I promised my vows to you. I intend to keep *my* word to you. Aren't *you* going to hold me to my word? Therefore, why would I not keep my word to God? How could you *possibly* think that I would not keep my word to God? Why would you make this more difficult for me than it already is?"

"Because you *can't* stop working!"

For the first time, I saw the fear on his face and heard the angst in his voice. He continued, "You cannot stop working because we need the income, and God knows that. Just look at the facts. If you stop working, we are going to lose half our income. Yet we will have to feed another mouth on that half income. If two of us are just barely making it with the two incomes we now have, how are we ever going to manage with half the income for three people?"

Ahhh, there it was. The truth was coming out. We had not really had a chance to talk about things since receiving the good news; we had merely made assumptions. We had not talked about the changes and the sacrifices we were going to have to make – as individuals, as a couple, and now, as a family – or the way either one of us felt about how it would impact us. I guess that for almost four years we had gotten into a comfortable routine with each other and our work. We had been praying for a miracle, and now that God had answered our prayer and granted us our miracle, we had not really talked about it or processed the miracle that was becoming our reality. We had not stopped to talk about how it was going to change our world as we knew it.

I understood Jack's feelings, his logic, and from where he was coming, but at that moment, I felt angry and unsupported. God had answered our earnest prayer, and now we were finding obstacles and making excuses for not being able to keep my word! I felt like such an ingrate with God. Worse yet, how could Jack possibly think that we could not keep our word to God? My incredulity left me speechless! All I could do was cry from a sense of frustration and helplessness.

Reflecting on it objectively, it must have taken a lot of courage for Jack to share what he did with me. He had totally exposed his emotions and his fears, and this *did* take a lot of courage. In addition, this was not just about me and *my* feelings and emotions. I had not bothered to take the time to ask him *his* feelings or *his* thoughts. As beautiful and wonderful as our miracle was, there were going to be major changes for both of us, not just me. I realized that I had been self-centered. I had focused on what I wanted and had neglected to consider Jack's thoughts and feelings, his dreams and desires, and his joys and his fears.

I was not the only one making sacrifices. Jack, too, had to make sacrifices – about the future and about our new reality. Quite frankly, we had failed to save money while we could have; we had lived for the moment. And even though we did not yet know it, we would one day realize and have to confess that we had not been good stewards – of our time, our talent, *or* our treasure, something for which we now know we will one day have to answer and to give account to the One who gives it all to us. In the meantime, I thank God that He has helped us to grow and to change for the better.

As I mentioned previously, at that time, my husband and I were "bench-warming" churchgoers. (I now like to think of ourselves as "heart-warming" churchgoers.☺) You could say we had our faith *in* God, but we certainly did not have a relationship *with* God. Nonetheless, I felt that Jack did not realize what he was saying. Nor did *I* fully comprehend things well enough to understand the magnitude of what God had done for us. I had not even begun to think about what He was going to do with us, for us, to us, through us, and in spite of us. All I knew was that I had to explain to my husband my desire to keep my word to God, and I had to convince him that I HAD to do it. Unfortunately, I did not know how to do that. I was not spiritually mature enough. I had not ever experienced God in this way or been up close and personal enough with Him to explain to my husband something that I did not fully comprehend myself.

8

My love for God in those days was certainly not what my love for Him is today. It couldn't be. Back then, it was a love that you have for anyone in general. We are to love everyone, so surely, I would love *Him*. You cannot love someone profoundly and unconditionally that you don't know personally and intimately, even if that someone has loved *you* unconditionally because *He* knows you and loves you. I did not have the words to lovingly and tenderly explain to my husband why I felt so strongly about this and why I knew that it was the right thing to do, at ALL levels, to keep my word to God. All I could do was to tell him that I was going to do it, no matter what.

I praise God for my husband – that his love for me and his trust in me was so great that he acquiesced to my desire and to my will. I thank God that He had given my husband the eyes to see me in a better light than I could ever see myself and that he trusted in me more than I did in myself. I thank God that my husband gave me the freedom and the ability to act on what I thought was right and best – to leave my job. He just wanted to know *how* I was going to do it. I told him that I did not know how, but that I was going to do it.

I started to talk more to God, to pray more. I asked Him for His help. I asked Him to show me, to teach me, how to be obedient to Him. Thank God that He knows the desires of our hearts; I know that He knew mine. I knew that I had to act quickly – that I had to let my co-workers and my superiors know that I was going to have a baby (most of them knew that my husband and I yearned to be able to have a family) and that I was going to be leaving my job. The truth is, I did not know where or how to begin.

One fateful day soon after my husband had given me his blessing to leave my job, I was driving and looking at the road between tears streaming down my cheeks, as the raindrops fell gently on the windshield of my car. My spirit was in anguish. I knew that leaving my job was going to change our lives forever. Perhaps it did not seem like a big deal to anyone else, but *I* knew it would be life-changing and transforming. I knew my life would be different, but I had no clue as to *how* different it was going to be.

My heart ached, my spirit ached, and my eyes hurt from so much crying. I knew that whatever I did in this situation was going to have a long-lasting impact on me ... on my husband, on our child, on our family, and on our future. It would forever change our lives. My decision would determine if we would continue to live where we did or if we would move to another city; this alone would impact the rest of our lives and would determine so much more. We were at a "Y" or "fork" junction of our lives, and what I decided next would determine which path in the road of life our family would take. I felt burdened with that responsibility, but I knew what I was going to have to do. I just did not know how I was going to go about doing it.

On that fateful and unforgettable day, I entered through the back door of my office hoping to go unnoticed. I asked the secretary to hold all my calls; I did not want to be disturbed until I collected myself. I had to get myself together. I barely had the emotional or physical strength to walk inside my office, but somehow, I did. I threw my belongings onto the chrome loveseat (yes, I am dating myself) in my office and fell to my knees in front of the armchair, but not before looking quickly around at my humble office. It was decorated with the things with which I had chosen to surround myself in the place where I spent so much of my time. I was going to miss this place – my office (and second home), the staff, the people whom we served – EVERYTHING! As I knelt and placed my head on my arms in front of that chair, I sobbed. "God, please help me. Hear my prayers. You helped me already and you heard my prayers when I asked you to let me get pregnant. Now *PLEASE* help me to know how to keep my end of the bargain, how to keep my word to You. You know how much I want to do that, I just don't know how. I feel scared. I don't know how to quit, how to resign, how to say good-bye, how to walk away from it all. Lord, I need You."

Suddenly, my phone intercom rang. I was surprised, because I had asked the secretary to hold all my calls. Feeling somewhat perturbed, I got up off the floor and walked over to my desk. It was in front of the only office window.

As I walked to my desk, I pulled the desk chair out and to the left side of my desk, moving it completely out of my way and next to the phone, which was also on the left side of my desk. I stood in front of my desk. My back was to the window and the chair was to my left facing me. I picked up the phone and asked the secretary why she had buzzed me when I had asked her specifically to hold my calls, something I don't recall ever having done before. She apologized profusely. She explained that the "boss" in our central office was on the line and had asked to speak to me, saying that it was very important. I assured her that it was okay that she had done that, but to please ask that person to give me a minute.

I composed myself and picked up the line, and after the typical pleasantries to one another, he proceeded to say, "Maria, I am afraid I am calling you with some bad news."

"Yes, what is it?"

"You know that we have had budget cuts and that we are going to have to shut down two of our offices, right?"

"Yes, I am aware of that. I am prepared to help do whatever is necessary to help our affected offices and staff with the transition. I know it won't be easy for them, but please count on me to do anything that I can to help to make this transition as painless and as easy as possible for all concerned."

We had already been notified that there was a RIF (reduction in force) in our agency. We had lost some funding, and we could no longer sustain our four regional offices. We were not worried in *our* particular Center because of the size of our own office. I was worried about the two smaller offices. What would they do? Where would they go?

"Well, I just wanted you to hear it from me that yours is going to be the first office to close."

Up to that point, I was ready to respond and offer suggestions of how to move staff around, of how I could go to the affected offices and help consolidate files, merge records, and any other administrative work. I **NEVER**, *EVER* expected to hear the words he had just said ... or, had I imagined them? I asked him, "What did you just say?" The shock that I felt was evident in the sound of my voice.

"Yours is the first office to close," he repeated.

All of a sudden, I realized that I was SEEING GOD AT WORK, firsthand, for the very first time. Everything got blurry. I could no longer hear what he was saying. I had not processed what I had just heard.

God again had heard and answered my prayers. Leaving my job ... *I* couldn't do it ... but *HE* could ... and He did! A bunch of things happened all at once. The room started to spin all around me. The phone dropped from my hand and my legs buckled under me. From far away, I looked down on what was happening. I knew I was going to fall, and I could do nothing to stop it. Everything seemed to happen as if in slow motion, as if I were on the outside looking in at everything that was happening.

All I could think of and say to myself was, "My baby." Mine was a high-risk pregnancy, and I was doing everything possible to take care of my unborn baby and myself. It was of no use. I was starting to fall. I was keenly aware that I had moved my desk chair to the side of me, and that I would be falling to the floor. I could do nothing to prevent the fall. I braced myself to hit the floor and for my head to hit the wall or window behind me.

I felt and I saw myself falling. There was not much distance between my upright position and the floor (I'm not a very tall person). The last thing I remember saying was, ***"God, please protect my baby!"***

What happened next is something that to this day I cannot wrap my head around. All I know is that I experienced firsthand the true meaning of grace and divine intervention. The next thing I knew was that I had fallen into my chair. I was not sure what had just happened. I ***KNEW*** the chair was to my side and not to my back. I ***KNEW*** that I should have fallen to the ground. I ***KNEW*** that there was nothing *humanly* possible that could have prevented me from falling to the ground. I **KNEW** there was the possibility that my baby could be injured with my fall. I realize now that *who* I ***DID NOT KNOW***, was **G O D**! I did not know the extent of His faithfulness, His goodness, His love, His grace, His protection, His mercy ***OR*** His sovereignty. Nor did I personally know the reach of His power. Sadly and interestingly, I did not even know or realize, until that precise moment, the depth of His love for me personally. ***Truly*** – what amazing, humbling, and awesome grace to experience firsthand!

In just a few seconds, God had manifested Himself to me in a major and profound way – twice, at that. He had showed me that He, indeed, was God. In those seconds, He showed me that *and* so much more. He showed me that **He *is* alive** and that **He *is* real**. He showed me that **He *really, truly* knows who *I* am**; furthermore, He showed me that **He really** and **truly** does care about me. He showed me just how much He loves me. That moment transformed me ***FOREVER***. God was my hero. He did what I could not do with my job, <u>*and*</u> He protected our baby. After all, He had given me this baby, and now, He had protected it and kept it safe. How could I ask for anything more or anything else? I wept, but now with different emotions.

This supernatural and divine experience seemed to take me to different realms of realization. It felt like time had stood still . . . like I were personally experiencing God in a profound way . . . as if He were there just for me.

Suddenly, I became aware of a small voice in the background. I could barely make it out. Then I realized that I had dropped the receiver and that the caller on the phone who had just dropped the bombshell on me was inquiring if I were alright. I quickly picked up the phone and apologized to him. I did not tell him what had just happened. I merely thanked him for personally letting me know. I don't remember exactly what we said after that, but I know it was some polite conversation about what it was we had to do to begin to bring closure to the office.

9

That day is a day I will remember for the rest of my life. It was the day of my powerful personal and spiritual conversion. It was that day that I offered my life to Christ. That I intentionally told God that I wanted to surrender control of my life to Him. That I told God that I wanted Him to come into my heart, to live there, and to take possession of my life and especially of my heart. It was that day that I became a new person, a new life in Christ Jesus, the day that I became what I now know to be a born-again Catholic Christian. I did not know the words for it then. I didn't even know or fully understand what had happened. I just knew that something wonderful and exciting and memorable had taken place. It would be years before I would come to understand and to know, and that God would help me realize, what He had done for me, both with this entire experience, as well as with what He had done on the Cross – for me, *AND* for you.

There were few goodbyes and some tears (mostly mine). All necessary arrangements had been made for staff who chose to transfer to one of the other offices, including the remaining smaller one. How ironic. What a sense of humor has our God!

Files were consolidated, keys turned in, appropriate furniture and supplies had been transferred to other offices and everything else was disposed of, dispensed with, or dispersed. Jack had asked the state agency for which he worked to transfer him to the main office located in Indianapolis. Now he and I headed there to start a new adventure that would take us on the longest spiritual journey of our lives, individually, as a couple, and as a family.

The Lord would take us to Indianapolis. Ironically, when it came time for us to close our office and to leave the area, I don't recall much fanfare taking place. I don't recall mobs of people coming to our front door to bid us farewell or to thank us for the years of service to them. I don't recall beloved colleagues, mine or Jack's, coming to shake our hands, or to say goodbye. I don't even recall my own staff conveying parting words of love or of gratitude, words of good wishes or anything else. We closed the doors to our office, just as Jack and I had closed the doors to our apartment and closed the pages to that chapter of our lives. Then we drove off.

Remember the baby shower I told you that I had wanted so badly? When we first learned that we were going to have a baby, I'll have to say that *everyone* was very excited for us. We lived in a relatively small town; nonetheless, there were many groups of people (friends, clients, colleagues) who had said they were going to throw a baby shower for Jack and me. I was thrilled! I love parties, and I love gifts, both to give and to receive, but mostly to give. I was excited about each of the baby showers I was told I would have. After moving away, I did not hear from any one of those groups or individuals, all those people who couldn't be happier for us and who couldn't wait to have a baby shower for us! I chuckle now as I think about it. I learned that people will disappoint us and that they sometimes don't keep their word, but that God is *ALWAYS* constant and faithful and that He **A L W A Y S** keeps His word.

Looking back on that now, I think it was a lesson God wanted me to experience and to learn, as He started to meld me, mold me, refine me, and fill me, so that He could use me – in *His* way and in *His* time. The **Life Lesson learned** was that our full reliance has to be on God and not on people. He will put people there for us to help us along the way, but HE is the One who we can fully trust and count on!

10

So there I was, pregnant, trying to figure out how I was going to "create" my own baby shower in a new city where I knew very few people. When the church bulletin that I mentioned earlier asked if one wanted to meet people, God planted the seed for me to attend that weekend of renewal. I found myself once again having to pay (God) a price for something I wanted; I had to do something that I did not necessarily want to do. However, it was a price I was prepared to pay; the price was to do something I normally would not have done. I would have NEVER guessed it would have such a life-changing impact. I was going to do something that would stretch me well beyond my comfort zone, and the outcome would have results beyond my greatest imagination and comprehension. The outcomes would be many, and varied, and would include transformed lives ... and joy ... and NISE ... and even this book. *I* did not know any better, but ***God*** did.

The small group of women that attended the weekend of renewal with me, of whom I also spoke earlier, threw me that baby shower I had wanted.

Maria C. Pimentel-Gannon

Yes, God let me receive what I had wanted, though it was not quite how I had imagined it. The shower was lovely, and it was small. More importantly, it was **simple** ... and there was much genuine and agape (unconditional and complete) love. I am still very grateful for this group of women, all of whom would become close friends to my family and me.

This experience was what I had referred to when I spoke of God's sense of humor and the lessons He wants us to learn. I had wanted a baby shower, so I asked God to let me meet women in enough time to interest them in throwing a shower for me; He gave me what I requested. Although I had envisioned a bigger shower, I got the perfect one. We need to say what we mean and mean what we say. I did not specify the size of shower I was requesting. In His wisdom, God let me experience relationships and friendships and simple love through these ladies and through the shower. This is what I needed more than I needed gifts, and God knew it, even though I did not. The **Life Lessons learned** here were: to appreciate what you get, even if it differs from your expectations; to be specific about what it is you are requesting; to look for the **golden nuggets** in every situation; and to be sure to learn from and value each experience. Those who learn from their experiences can easily repeat or avoid those experiences, depending what outcome they want. What I needed more than gifts were friends, companions on my journey, and love. God saw to it that I got what I needed, while still giving me some of what I wanted. And I learned sincere gratitude and appreciation for the simple things in life.

A few months after moving to Indianapolis, Jack and I had a pleasant surprise. Much to our joy, one of his friends who worked with him (both she and her husband worked with Jack, and Jack was friends with both; they would later also become friends of mine) said that she and some of their colleagues wanted to throw us a baby shower. And they did. And it was a BIG one. It was held in our friend's lovely home. And we received a bunch of gifts.

And so it was, God used many acquaintances and strangers to me, some of whom would later become dear friends, to give me the desire of my heart, worldly as it (my desire) was at that time – to throw this shower for us (it was a couples' shower). Everything was so lovely; I was deeply touched and overcome with gratitude and humility at experiencing God's faithfulness yet once again. Through this experience, I learned another **Life Lesson**: God remembers the desires of our heart. He may not give them to us when we want them, but we can rest assured that He will give them to us in His perfect time . . . as long as it is in accordance with His will and His plan for us.

God showed me a few key things through this baby shower incident. First of all, He showed me that He indeed has a sense of humor. I had wanted a baby shower so badly, and He gave me one – a small one. He showed me that He is merciful; he allowed me to also have a big baby shower, to make lots of new friends, and to receive lots of gifts. God showed me that we need to be content in all things and in all of our circumstances. **Life Lesson learned**: if we learn contentment with little blessings, God can then bless us with more. He taught me that even when we mean something for one reason, He intends it for another. (Genesis 50:20) I had gone on this "spiritual" weekend to meet people for the purpose of getting a baby shower and gifts out of it, but His purpose for my going on this weekend was different. He wanted me to have better gifts of a long-lasting kind.

God also taught me that it is not so much the number or the kind of gifts we receive or the attention we might get as the guests of honor. Rather, it is the *love* that goes behind the act of kindness. It is the same love that God had shown me before. It is also the same love that He has for **_ALL_** His children, whether we accept and receive the love or not.

The operative words here are "accept and receive or not." It is our choice. He gives us free will, so it is up to us whether we say yes or no. Either way, He still loves us. That is the beauty of it all. It's just like parents – whether our child acts like s/he loves us or not, or whether s/he says s/he loves us or not, we don't stop loving that child. Yet, in our humanity, *our* love is imperfect. But *God's* love is perfect. Too many times *our* love is conditional. "For our ways are not God's ways, nor are our thoughts His thoughts." We hear this in God's Holy Word in the Old Testament book of Isaiah in Chapter 55. And it is so true. **Life Lesson learned**: we cannot begin to imagine the depth or the width or the extent of God's unconditional love because we ourselves are not capable of that kind of love. Oh, that we would have that capability!

I will always remember our dear friends who worked so hard to make that baby shower very special for us: Maureen, who has battled cancer and who reached out to me and showed me unconditional love, even without knowing me, and Judy, who, with her robust and contagious laugh, made anyone who met her feel like they had known her for years. It was her love, as well, that made this possible. Maureen and Judy loved Jack, and because of him, they embraced me in their love, as well. Judy eventually succumbed to cancer many years ago, but her love and friendship will always be remembered. Maureen had continued to fight her battle with cancer through the years, and praise be to God, she had remained the victor for this long. It breaks my heart that before this book could be finally published, she lost her battle to this horrendous disease. It grieves me deeply that I never got the chance to let her know how much she meant to both Jack and me and to show her that she was publicly thanked in this book. The good news is that I can at least let her husband and kids know.

11

Jack and I adapted to Indianapolis. We started going to church more regularly, less out of obligation and more out of desire. After I went on my Christ Renews His Parish weekend, I was not sure that I had "experienced" what others thought (and hoped) we would experience. But I did feel grateful, nonetheless. I felt loved. It was the first time that I had felt loved like that by anyone other than Jack. Even my extended family was not one to display that kind of love. It was a good feeling – to feel loved by strangers in the world, although not strangers in Christ. It brought about change in me. It was not anything dramatic or sudden. Rather, it was a slow and steady change. I was subconsciously aware of it, but nothing more. However, my husband noticed it.

One day, shortly before my daughter was born, I was sitting on our bed reading through some cards and letters I had received while on that weekend that would be part of my continued transformation. I was still trying to digest how people who didn't even know me (nor did I know who they were) could write me such genuine, heartfelt letters filled with so much love. I was touched in a way I had never before been touched. It moved me beyond what words could describe. I had never experienced such a weekend. Except from my husband, I had never experienced the kind of unconditional love that I did on that weekend, and certainly not from strangers.

As I sat on the bed and told myself that I was so fortunate to have gone on this weekend, that I had gotten so much more out of it than I had expected, my husband walked in. I remember looking up at him lovingly, with a smile on my face; I am confident that my smile conveyed the deep and abiding love that I was feeling for him at that very moment. He approached the bed and leaned over on it. He asked me what I was doing. I told him that I was just reading. I was not supposed to tell him much about the weekend; those weekends are filled with so many surprises for the participants. He knew that I had received "stuff" because he had been asked to write me a letter, but he did not know more than that. I had just finished reading the letter of love and affirmation that he had sent me. I told him how blessed I felt to have him in my life and that I could not wait until our child was born to be able to be a family that went from two to three. I told him that I just knew he would make a wonderful father; he already was the perfect husband for me. Through the years, many friends have told me that they wished he could be cloned – that the world needed more men like him. I agree, even today, after thirty-six years of marriage at the time this book was printed.

Suddenly, he took my hands in his and he looked into my eyes. With gentleness he said, "Mari, I don't know what happened to you, what you experienced on that weekend. You've changed. You're different now. You radiate peace and serenity. You seem to have a special maturity and confidence about you. Your face seems to glow with beauty and joy. There seems to be an aura around you. I can't quite put my finger on it, but I can see it, and I can sense it. Whatever it is, I want it. I want to have the same thing that you have. I want to experience whatever has brought about this change in you."

I looked at him and just said, "I cannot explain it. All I can say is that I got to know God a little bit better when all of this happened about getting pregnant, about letting go of my job, about keeping my word to God, and about being obedient. I feel that God is reaching out to me wanting me to know Him even more deeply and more personally. I know I surrendered my life to Him when all of this happened at the office and He let me experience the depth and height of his love, but I feel like He wants more than that. I feel like He wants to use me."

Then Jack responded, "If that is the case, then I want to be on that journey with you. I know I did not want you to leave your job. I know that I wanted you to stay there because of the money. But if this is what God wants from us, then I want to do it. I want to help you keep your promise. I know we won't have the money we want, but I believe we'll have what we need. I just want to grow old with you with our child at our side. I want us to be a family."

That was a pivotal time in our lives. I shall never forget that moment or the love between us, or how that moment felt. I believe that was a turning point, not just in our life, but also in our marriage. Before our daughter was born, we did not know whether we would have a daughter or a son. Not like today, where you can find out everything you want to know – and sometimes things you don't want to know – before the child is born. What we did know was that we would love our child unconditionally. Perhaps we would have only one child, but we were going to make the best of it. When the day came that we had our child, that I held my daughter in my hands for the very first time – that was the day that I saw the face of God, in my child and in my husband.

I will always remember the look on my husband's face when he held our daughter, our Jacqueline, in his arms for the very first time. I don't know for whom the look of love was the greatest – for his wife or for his child. It didn't matter; I just reveled in the beauty and the sacredness of the moment. God was using ALL of this to prune us, to refine us, to mold us, and to fill us . . . so that He could use us, in His time and for His purpose.

12

Soon after Jacqueline was born, my husband was in a state of trying to discern direction for his life. He did not know what he wanted out of life, he just knew he wanted more. He talked to me about the possibility of going to law school. He was not sure because of the expense and the time involved. It had always been my own dream to go to law school, but even though it had been my dream, I don't think it was God's plan for me. Early in my life, I had been a paralegal, but that would probably be the extent of my legal profession. I encouraged him to "pray about it," both about direction for his life and about law school in particular. It is interesting how comfortable I was beginning to feel with those words, with that kind of help and advice. How easily it flowed from my mouth, how comfortable I was talking in a way that at one time would have been foreign to me, and how genuine and natural the thoughts and feelings and words were. I was very aware that God was taking me on this special journey.

Jack prayed about it, and we prayed together. He applied and got accepted – the good news. The bad news was that I hardly ever saw him, and Jacqueline never saw him except for brief moments on the weekend. By this time Jacqueline was two years old. This change was hard on her because Jack used to spend a lot of time with her. They were good buddies, and clearly, she was Daddy's little girl, but now, she hardly ever saw him. She would be asleep in the morning when he left for work, since he would get to the office early, and she would be asleep at night when he got home, since he went straight to class and/or to the library after work. One Saturday at the dinner table when we were eating together, she would not look at or acknowledge him, even when he tried talking to her. I asked her what was wrong. Out of nowhere our two-year-old daughter said in a matter-of-fact tone, "My daddy doesn't live here anymore." Jack's jaw dropped, and the hurt and sadness he was feeling was all over his face. The following Monday, Jack went to school and changed from a four-year to a five-year program. To this day, our now-attorney daughter remembers what her dad did for her.

I got involved quickly at church. After going on the weekend of renewal, I learned that they needed help with the church bulletin because the church secretary, Marie, who happened to be one of my "sisters" on my Christ Renews His Parish team, was retiring. I had the time, I loved to write, and I loved to type, so why not. I offered to help and they gladly accepted my help. Soon after I would become the Bulletin Editor, much to my pleasant surprise. God was going to give me a taste of the joy of writing.

Soon after becoming the Bulletin Editor, when the school year was about to start, I heard that the Religious Education department needed a Sunday School teacher. I "prayed about it" and I ended up teaching the high school seniors that year. Since then, I have been part of the Religious Education program in one aspect or another, and since 1999 or so, I have been the Coordinator of the Hispanic Religious Education program at our church.

Once again, God showed that He has a sense of humor. I had never gone to a Catholic or other Christian school. I had the necessary Sunday School preparation for me to receive the Sacraments and to help me to learn the Baltimore Catechism, but that was the extent of my "religious" education and knowledge. Fortunately, I had grown up in a home where my mother taught us to pray – every night – to read the Bible, and to have unfailing faith. With those tools, I began to teach my first religious education class. Since then,

God has equipped me through courses on theology, studies on the Bible and church teachings, and a plethora of workshops and trainings on faith, religion, the Church, spirituality, etc. And He has used me to be a spiritual guide to a multitude of people. God has used this unworthy servant to help others to better know Him and to draw closer to Him. I am so incredibly humbled and blessed to be used by God in this way!

13

"God has prepared you for such a time as this." (Esther 4:14) I *now* know this scripture that is found in the book of Esther, though I did not know it then. I still did not know how God "worked." I just knew that He was up to something in my life. Back when I was a college student, I had the "head knowledge" that I was a Christian because I believed in and knew Jesus Christ as my Lord and Savior, but I had not yet surrendered my life to Him. I did not yet have a personal relationship with the Lord. The term "born again" was foreign to me. I had only heard it on campus. Friends had told me to "watch out for those 'Jesus freaks,'" for those born-again Christians, for those Bible-thumpers who were "out to get you." I was told that they were called evangelists.

I did not know what they looked like or how to identify them if I did see them. All I knew was that I had to watch out for them. It was around this time that I started hearing the name Billy Graham. I did not know who he was, nor did I know anything else about him, but I knew that they called him one of the greatest evangelists ever, so I knew that I had to watch out for him and for any of his kind.

I remember the very first time I heard someone standing on campus speaking loudly about repenting, about giving your life to God, about being born again, and about having a personal relationship with Jesus Christ. I did not know what all of that meant, but I knew that that boy was one of those "Jesus freaks" of which I had been warned. I remember I told one of my "friends" at the time that I had encountered a "Jesus freak," but that I had managed to avoid him. I was thankful that I had been warned about them.

In His sense of humor, God would one day in the future have someone yell at me at a time when I was being kind to her. This person could not understand that I was helping her unconditionally, and that I expected nothing in return. She yelled at me, telling me to get my "Jesus freak" self out of her way! I still laugh to this day!

Sadly, I started to see that there was a division in people who say they love God. Supposedly, God loves ALL people, yet those people who wanted to tell others of God's love seemed to want to reach out only to people who looked like them, thought like them, sounded like them, and/or believed like them.

When Jacqueline was very little, not quite yet two years of age, I was invited to an international

Bible study. But when I got to the Bible study and they learned that I was a Catholic Christian, the people just weren't as friendly as they had been before knowing the denomination to which I belonged. I did not understand. As it turned out, I could not join the Bible study group because of lack of childcare, so that took care of my dilemma, at least for the time being. It would not be until several years later that I would be able to take advantage of going to this wonderful Bible study that seemed to be changing for the better.

14

One day, after dealing with bronchitis for a while, I went back to the doctor (thank the Lord, Jack was with me this time), only to be told that I was pregnant. I was in shock. I could not believe my good fortune. God truly *did* love me. He was blessing me with another child. How could life get any better than this?!? Jack and I did not believe in knowing the gender of our child before birth (and the opportunity to know it was not as available as it is today), but I knew in my heart that it was a boy. I was so excited. My little Jacqueline would have her baby brother. She would only be about 18 months or so when her brother would be born. This is why it shocked me to learn that I was pregnant . . . and so quickly! Even though we had been told that we would not be able to conceive, we were blessed twice: with our first daughter and now with this second pregnancy – and so soon after the birth of our first child! Wow! It just did not get any better than that. I told my husband my suspicions about the baby being a boy. Of course, he was elated because he knew that I often had intuition that was right on target.

I was again taking precaution with my pregnancy. I did not want to do anything to jeopardize the birth of my son. I had always heard that there is nothing more special than the bond between a son and a mother. Of course, I had also heard that there is no greater love than that between a daughter and her father. All I knew was that there was going to be a lot of love going around our household!

A little bit before my sixth month of pregnancy, I started spotting and I started having some pain; I thought they could be Braxton Hicks contractions. I did not give it much thought, but it did concern me a little. Nothing else happened, so I let it go. Then at my next doctor's visit, another doctor happened to see me instead of my regular doctor. We were chatting and he was asking me how things were going. He was telling me how much he enjoyed these visits with moms-to-be because they were always so happy and excited about the life that was growing inside each one of them.

I told him how I was convinced that we were having a boy. As we spoke, he kept listening to my tummy with his stethoscope. You could tell he was no longer fully listening to what I was saying, but that he was listening closely into his stethoscope. Then he did an ultrasound. I kept making small talk, but he had gotten rather quiet by then. When I finally took notice of the change in the atmosphere of our visit, I asked him if he were okay, to which he of course said, "Sure." Then he said he would be right back. He said that he thought he heard my doctor in the hallway and that he would go check. After a while, my doctor came into the examination room. He said very little, and he started to check me the way the first doctor had been checking me.

He started asking me questions like what had I been doing, how had I been feeling, had I noticed anything different in the baby, etc. I answered his questions, told him about the spotting, and I told him how active the baby had been recently. He had been kicking up a storm. The doctor kept adjusting his stethoscope as he listened to my belly. I asked him what was wrong. By now, the nonverbal cues and the body language communicated to me that something was amiss. He told me he had bad news. He said the baby's heartbeat could not be detected. I told him that the baby must be asleep because earlier that morning my son had been acting as if he were carrying on a one-man soccer game.

The heartbreak of my life would come when it was confirmed that my baby was dead. Something had happened, and my son whom I had come to know and love and watch grow in my belly was gone. My spirit ached, and my heart was shattered in pieces. Had I not been in such shock and grief, I would have named him. Had we named him, his name probably would have been Zachariah Isaiah or Caleb Zachariah or Jeremiah Isaiah or Isaiah Rory. Those were the names we had talked about and considered. In any case, he'll always be my baby boy. At that moment, the fact that God's Son had died as well, as a living sacrifice for us, came to mind. Thinking about this only increased my love and appreciation for God, while helping to ease the deep and profound ache in my heart.

15

By now, I had started teaching part time. I taught Spanish to preschoolers and to elementary school students. I LOVED teaching. What I loved more than that was that I could take my daughter with me, and she could learn what I was teaching.

It would be around 18 months after we lost our son that I would experience my second huge miracle – the birth of my beautiful and precious second daughter, Veronica. My little Veronica showed me, while in utero, the depth of her will. My Jacqueline weighed 9 pounds 3 ounces. My Veronica, never one to be outdone, weighed in at 9 pounds 13 ounces. She arrived via caesarean because even after a most painful attempt to "turn her around" a few weeks earlier at a doctor's appointment, she did not want to move from her breached position.

My Jacqueline was a beautiful baby, born with blue eyes and blond hair; she did not have as much hair as her little sister, but they both now have tons of beautiful hair. My Veronica, also a beautiful baby, was born with dark eyes and a head full of black hair. Jacqueline was the proudest big sister. As a matter of fact, when Veronica came into this world (both were born very early in the morning, 5:30 and 4:30, respectively), Jacqueline burst into the room and marched right up to the bed where Veronica was snuggled in my arms. Her blond curls swinging over her favorite green hooded top and her pants, she demanded, "Where's my baby sista!?!"

She reached out and almost snatched her baby sister out of my arms. Jacqueline was a few weeks shy of her third birthday, and she thought she was all grown up. We wanted to be careful how we handled that kind of situation because we did not want to scare her by overreacting whenever she attempted to carry her "baby sista" or to make her feel that we loved her baby sister more; nor did we want her to feel slighted or jealous. We wanted it to be the best experience for her to be a big sister. We had been practicing with dolls while I was pregnant, so she could "help me" with the baby. We gently took Baby Veronica from her arms and placed her back into mine. That was that. She was done. The novelty had worn off for the moment. "Now what?" Her dad and I could only laugh to hear her declare those words as she looked around the hospital room. Little did we know then that she would grow up to be the best big sister the world could ever produce! She has always been kind and loving and protective of her little sister. Not that they didn't ever fight or argue, but boy, just don't let anyone else threaten her sister!

Our little Veronica was born into a world filled with so much love for her. She was beautiful, and I am not saying that just because I'm her mom. Like her big sister, Jacqueline, she still is a beautiful young woman, inside and out.

Veronica was born with a rare type of skin cancer – a malignant melanoma, the doctor called it. We learned the depth of her strength and her courage, as well as her intelligence, at a very young age. Before she was 18 months, she had her first surgery. Seeing my baby girl with her head all bandaged made the tears that had gathered in my eyes want to flow forth. I fought hard to hold them back. I did not want to scare her nor did I want her to think that there was something wrong with her just because of the bandages covering her head. She looked like she was wearing a turban, and we used that to get her to feel special.

I will never forget how she clung to me, literally, as the nurses tried to peel her away from my arms when they were ready to take her into surgery. She had not cried much when they inserted the needle into her little arm to set up the IV, but she cried fiercely when they pulled her out of my arms. I felt like they were tearing my heart out! I was so scared for my daughter. Hearing her cry as they pried her fingers away from my blouse, and seeing her reach out to me as they took her away, tugged at every fiber of my motherly being. When she started yelling, "Mommy, mommy, I yuv you. Don't go. Pease, mommy don't go," my heart tore into a million little pieces. "God, please take care of my baby girl." I put on a brave facade in front of her; no sooner had the operating room doors closed when my own tears and sobs came fiercely. I pleaded with God once again; once again, he answered my prayers. This would happen a second time to our baby girl, and in His faithfulness and sovereignty, God would be with us through that ordeal, as well.

Around the time of her second surgery, we learned of Veronica's excellent memory. I had taken her to a day care center when she was a little over 2½ years of age. I had gone back to work on a temporary, part-time basis; I wanted to see if day care was the right fit for her. Jacqueline was already in kindergarten. Veronica went for a couple of days, but I decided that I did not want her at a day care; I wanted her in a place with fewer kids. I wanted her in a place where she would get more attention and where more visible love and prayer might prevail.

Shortly after having attended the day care, I heard her saying some words repeatedly but was not sure what she was saying. When I finally sat down with her and asked her to tell me what she was saying, she recited the Pledge of Allegiance. She had learned the Pledge in the very short time she had been at the day care. She looked so precious as she stood at attention with her hand across her chest and kept repeating the Pledge of Allegiance. "I pedge ayegiance to da flag ov da United Tates of Amewica . . ."

I was amazed. Both my husband and I could not believe our ears. We learned that our darling Veronica was a precocious child, and she was a little ham. She loved to recite the Pledge every chance she could, in front of any audience. She was not shy, and this lack of shyness has served her well in life. She still is very amazing, and she still has the amazing memory. Thank God for that, because when she reaches her mother's age, she will need all the help she can get to remember things! ☺

16

I have to share with you that Veronica helped me with something that I had started to do again after Jacqueline started school. I found myself craving cigarettes and every once in a while, I would light a cigarette and sneak a few puffs. Then I started buying a pack here and there. Of course, I did not want my family to see me smoke, but Veronica found out and, of course, she told her sister. Both expressed their disappointment in me. Jacqueline chastised me, repeating the things she had learned at school about drugs being bad for you.

I learned that I could do anything difficult for a greater cause and purpose. Since Veronica was more than three years old and still sucked her thumb, I made a deal with her. We had tried repeatedly to get her to stop sucking her thumb, trying all the things we knew and heard to do, but to no avail. I told her that I would not smoke any more cigarettes if she would stop sucking her thumb. "Ever," she asked? How could this little girl, precocious as she was, even think to ask me that question! My word is my bond, so I thought before answering. "Okay, honey. I will stop smoking forever if you stop sucking your thumb. Smoking is not good for me, and sucking your thumb is not good for your teeth. Is it a deal?"

She thought for a moment. "Deal mommy," she finally said.

I kept my word. She tried to keep hers. Even though I caught her sucking her thumb on occasion (when falling asleep, etc.), I can attest that she has long since kept her word.

When Veronica got married at the age of 28 on the 4th of July, 2014, her dad had the honor of presiding over her wedding ceremony, and her best friend and sister, Jacqueline, was her maid of honor. Her destination wedding in my home country of Mexico was the picture-perfect site for this beautiful young lady's marriage to Peter. Jack and I were in bliss; ten uninterrupted days with our two precious daughters, a first in their adult lives. I am not sure why God blessed us with our two precious girls – they are His greatest gifts to us – but we are eternally grateful. Now He has blessed us with a son . . . a good son, and a good husband for Veronica. Thank You, Lord.

My family would experience the heartbreak of miscarriage yet another three times. However, we had our two special miracles, and we could not be more grateful. They were, are, and always will be our greatest joys. If it is true that even our unborn children are in heaven, I will one day have the big family of which I had dreamed. I know that through my own experiences of miscarriage, I have been able to minister to other people who are coping with the loss of births through miscarriage, stillbirth, infant death, and even abortion. God truly uses ALL things for the good of those who know Him, love Him, and have been called according to His purpose. (Romans 8:28)

17

In my journey through life, God is having me do lots of ecumenical work. I am involved with people of all denominations and of many faiths. I even have a plethora of Baptist and other evangelical friends. God *does* have a sense of humor, as I've mentioned earlier. He had me work on a project with the Billy Graham crusade, and while I did not get to personally meet him, I felt that I connected with Reverend Graham. I believe that God wants me to write a letter to him or maybe just send him a copy of this book. I feel that I need to apologize to him for having scoffed at the work that he does and for having laughed in my heart at "Jesus freaks" and other evangelists.

The truth is that when Reverend Graham openly talked about loving one another as children of God, regardless of which church the person is a part of, I was able to see him with different eyes. I saw him as a true, Godly man. I knew, and still know, that I was to write him that letter and that I was to explain some things to him. Will that ever happen in either of our lifetimes? I don't know, but if it is God's will, then indeed, it will happen.

Maria C. Pimentel-Gannon

Just recently, I helped to work on his daughter's event when she came to town. It was a very good experience, and I am so glad to have been a part of that endeavor, particularly since historically, the Catholics and the Evangelicals had not held one another in high esteem, and each thought they were going to be the only ones who would be in heaven. Now, there is more and more camaraderie between these two groups of believers, as well as among other Christian groups. I will have the opportunity to work on Billy's son's crusade, when and if he comes to Indianapolis. God bless this family and the many ways He is working with, through, for, and in spite of them.

Knowing what our gifts are is truly a gift in itself. Receiving confirmation and affirmation of those gifts from others is the icing on the cake. That is one of the beautiful things that came about as a result of my having gone on the Christ Renews His Parish weekend in March of 1983. For this experience, I am eternally grateful, and I mean that literally. Who would have ever known that God would use this Roman Catholic Mexican to bring others to Christ? Who would have ever known that this woman would tirelessly talk about God, about being born again, about surrendering one's life to Christ, and would "evangelize" anyone God would put in her path. In a million years, I would not have been able to imagine or predict it. Just another example of God's sense of humor and His mysterious ways. **Life Lesson learned**: God does not call the equipped and the prepared, but He will equip and prepare the called.

Another example of God's mysterious ways: who would have ever thought that my husband, a "gringo," would be used to minister to Hispanic men, to teach them about God, and to bring them to a personal relationship with Him, even though he is not fluent in Spanish? This truly is a vivid and living example of that precious golden nugget and life lesson I just shared – "**God does not call the equipped, but He equips the called**." He called Jack, and He equipped him, and somehow, through the years, with the Spanish Jack knew and the English that the men who God put in his path knew, God allowed transformation to happen, both for Jack, as well as for the men. **Life Lesson learned**: we don't have to have ability to be used by God, only **availability**. We must have the desire to avail ourselves to be used by God for His greater purpose!

This brings to mind yet another example of God's sense of humor. I did eventually rejoin the same Bible study in which I had at one time felt unwelcome because of my denomination. Attending Bible study and spending time working on my Bible study homework took my attention away from my then growing daughters. Jacqueline, in particular, complained that I was always doing my Bible study homework and not being attentive to them. She was very family oriented and loved to spend time together as a family; to this day, love of family is one of her greatest attributes.

A few years back, when she finished her undergraduate degree, she was part of the Alliance for Catholic Education (ACE) program out of the University of Notre Dame, where she also attended college. Through this program, she taught third grade in inner city Dallas for a couple of years. One evening I was talking with her on the phone when suddenly she told me she had to hang up because she had arrived where she was going that evening. When I asked her where that was, she told me she was going to her Bible study (the same study for which she had given me grief when she was younger). I did not know if I should laugh or cry; in either case, it would have been out of sheer joy for her having said "yes" to God's call to Bible study. After Veronica moved to California, she, too, joined the same Bible study. God's sense of humor never ceases to put a smile on my face.

God has been manifesting Himself in my life and that of my family in many, many ways through that sense of humor and through His mysterious ways. He has blessed me beyond description and beyond anything imaginable. When Veronica was younger and still in high school, she became a little evangelist. She would go to Florida and other states to do beach evangelization, and she even shared her testimony via interpreter in the Czech Republic. How funny it was that the daughter of a woman, who at one point in her life laughed at evangelical activity, would not only be a part of that same activity, but would be making her mama proud for doing so. Of course, I have asked God to forgive me for my ignorant behavior and thoughts, and I've thanked Him for having allowed my daughter to walk in His footsteps.

That same daughter attended the church of another great evangelist in our country. She met Peter, fell in love with him, and married him; he is a good man, one who shares her love for the Lord. Together, they attend that church. I think that they have come to the Lord in a personal way, as a couple and as individuals. They have things to overcome, which we all do, but they both have God in their heart, so they have the most necessary ingredient. They go to church together, they pray together, and they love one another very much. I am so grateful to have Peter as a part of our family. I pray for them constantly, that they will overcome the temptations and the deceit of the enemy to deter them from their Godly path. I pray that Peter, as well as Jacqueline's future husband, would each be a man who knows, loves, and puts God first before all things, followed by his wife, then his children, and then everything else. This is the order that God intends.

18

After many years of having been part of the Christ Renews His Parish experience for English speakers, the time came to have something for Spanish speakers. The look of our city started to change in the late 90's. All of a sudden, we started getting a lot of people of Hispanic/Latino heritage, and many of them spoke only Spanish. The Indianapolis community moved quickly to address the issues arising from the increase in numbers of this population. Our church was no different. We needed to address the spiritual needs and growth of that segment of our community. We already had a wonderful process for experiencing personal and parish spiritual renewal for the English speakers of our congregation. Now we just had to offer it in Spanish.

By God's grace, the program was translated into Spanish and we were finally able to evangelize and minister to our parishioners whose first language is Spanish. We were the first to do it in our area. God blessed me with the opportunity to be part of the team to initiate it in our city. To this date, God continues to allow me to be part of this beautiful experience, including in other parishes and churches. The good news is that I no longer have to be the one to lead the groups. We have trained others to be leaders, and still others will be trained . . . all to the glory of God.

Remembering back to the time when we arrived in Indianapolis in 1982, I felt like something was missing, as if *I* were lacking something. I felt like something was missing from my church experience and from my spiritual growth and development. I was already on the road to personal ecumenism. I was visiting a lot of other churches. I thought that maybe God was calling me to a different church. The truth is that I was ready to leave. I wanted to be more scripture-oriented, to be a stronger and more authentic Catholic Christian, and to be more God-conscious, in practice and not just in word. I did not want my prayers to be rote; and I wanted my faith to stem from my relationship with God and not merely from tradition. I had become discontent with the place where I was spiritually. I didn't know any different church denomination; I had been born and raised in the Catholic Church, so for me to make that change would have been a major move.

At this point in time, I had one brother and one sister who had left the Catholic Church and joined nondenominational Christian churches, each for their own reasons. Another sister left in later years. To some Catholic Christians, there could be no sadder thing; to my mom, it had been devastating. I did not want to break my mother's heart yet one more time, but there had to be more to faith and spirituality than what I was then living and experiencing. Of course, I had not stopped to think at the time that no church is perfect and that every church has its strengths and its weaknesses. Plus, if the problem were my own problem, it would only be a matter of time before it would catch up with me, regardless of which church I were to attend. Just when I was convinced that leaving was what I wanted and needed to do, I became aware of the Lord's voice. He was asking me, "Who told you to leave [the Catholic Church]?" "Nobody," I said. "Then, where do you think you are going? *I* did not tell you to leave. I want you to remain where you are and to 'bloom where you are planted.' I want you to evangelize My people in the Catholic Church!"

There it was – that special word again: EVANGELIZE. Again, God was showing me His sense of humor and His mysterious ways. I knew nothing about evangelization ... but He did. I obeyed, and I stayed – we stayed. I don't know what would have happened to my marriage if God had not called me to evangelize in the Catholic

Church. My husband knows that I have been called to evangelize, but I don't think he ever thought that it might be outside the Catholic Church. We may never know what would have happened, but I am glad we don't have to find out. God had revealed to me one of His wonderful purposes for my life, and the truth is, I love my church, even in all its imperfections. To encounter God through other God-loving and God-fearing brothers and sisters, especially through the gift of the Eucharist, and to experience God in the journey of other born-again Catholic Christians, is something I never want to live without.

Once I decided to stay where God had placed me, that is, to remain in the Roman Catholic Church, I opened myself to Him, without realizing at the moment what I was doing. I tried to listen more attentively, more actively, more consciously, more intentionally. As is sung in the musical *Godspell*, I wanted to "see Him more clearly, love Him more dearly, follow Him more nearly . . . day by day." I felt that I was headed in that direction. I tried to hear His voice in the silence of the moment, as well as in the loudness of the hustle and bustle of my day.

I believe that if Satan cannot make you bad, he will make you busy, so I do not use the word "busy" for myself; rather, I use the word "active."

God keeps me *very* active – actively building His Kingdom. Indeed, my plate is very full, but only with what God wants to put on it to accomplish His purpose. That is what I realized. God is having me actively do things that continue to build His Kingdom here on earth. After all, I may have only one opportunity to make a difference; therefore, I must seize the moment.

As a very active person, I have to be mindful and conscious of what I am doing. When I put things on my planner (I am still a paper/hard copy person), I try to discern what it is that should go in there and what shouldn't. If it is not in God's plan for me to do it, I don't want it on there. Yet sometimes it does get on there. Therefore, I have to be in deeper prayer to be able to discern if it is a "me" thing or a "God" thing that causes it to be on there.

When I gave myself to the Lord that unforgettable and transformational day back in 1982 (when I experienced God's realness and when He showed me that He knew me personally), I did so mindful of the fact that the only thing that mattered to me was to do God's will and to fulfill His purpose for my life. Back then, and still today, I only want to do what He is guiding and directing me to do.

19

A beautiful golden nugget and **Life Lesson** that I learned while going through my renewal and transformation process is that "**there are no co- incidences in life, only God-incidences**." This is true even when it comes to my heritage. God has a purpose for my having been born in Mexico, for my being an immigrant, for my being Hispanic/Latino, and even for my being a woman. He has shown me a multitude of times why some things are the way they are.

I have shared with you that I have been part of the Religious Education program at my church since 1983, a year after having arrived in Indianapolis. I mentioned that for many years and since its inception, I have been the Coordinator of the Hispanic Religious Education program. One of the many wonderful things that resulted from this is that I have been able to teach. God's focus has been for me to teach not just the students, but the parents and the families, as well.

You see, what God let me realize is that "*we cannot learn what we were never taught, and we cannot teach what we never learned.*" Or another way to say this is that we (children and adults alike) learn what we live and live what we learn. And this **is** true. Illustratively, our faith denomination, like many others, has been one that is lived primarily out of tradition, obligation, habit, guilt, or other such motivation. Seldom was our faith lived out of our own personal relationship with God or from an experiential or biblical knowledge of God's Word. Nor was our faith and spirituality always built on being grounded in our biblical beliefs and our church's teachings. Therefore, most of us did not own our faith. It was borrowed – from our parents, from significant people in our lives, from tradition or habit, and even from our ancestry.

God wanted me to help my brothers- and sisters-in-Christ in the Roman Catholic Church to realize that they had to have their own personal relationship with Him. He wanted me to share with them what I had learned and experienced through my personal relationship with Him.

I learned that I have to personally invite Him to live in my heart. I have to want Him, to desire Him, to hunger for Him, to thirst for the living water that He offers me freely. I have to acknowledge for myself that I am a sinner, and I have to repent of those sins and to try to not sin any more. I have to invite Jesus to dwell in my heart, and to commit to Him, to let Him be Lord and Master of my life. He has to be my **first** **priority** – not one of many. He taught me that we *have* to be willing to live our lives according to God's plan and purpose, and not our own. We have to yield our will for our lives to God's will, and we have to live our lives in a way that demonstrates "**Whose we are by how we are.**" We have to desire the necessary ingredients for spiritual enlightenment. No, scratch that. I learned that I **GET** to do all these things once I invite Him into my heart. This sounds so complex, but it is not! If I truly love the Lord, and I am willing to accept His will for my life, what I've learned is that, because of the power of the Holy Spirit, what I have just shared with you is a simple thing to do.

God started this work in me when I came to this parish, after I had my born-again experience, after I learned of my pregnancy, and after I lost my job. I started to work with the Spanish-speaking families. I taught the students and the parents of the young people who had not received certain Sacraments (something integral to the Catholic Christian faith), but who had reached a certain age. God continued to show me that I had a love for teaching; He also showed me that He had given me a wonderful gift to teach. I knew that there was something that made my classes extra special. The fact that I was bilingual and bicultural gave me credibility with both the parents and the students. And the fact that I love the Lord with ALL my heart, soul, mind and might made my love for teaching these classes even more special and more appealing to me (and to them). Through all the classes that I have taught, and throughout the many years I have taught, God has made it a very, very rewarding experience for me.

I feel that *I* have been the one to benefit from my teaching experiences. I have learned a lot about myself since 1982, and I realize that *I* have grown by leaps and bounds. I have become more pliable material in the hands of the Great Potter, and I am a work in progress. My growth has not only been spiritual, but it has been personal. I know that I am a much, much better person because of the opportunity to teach these special families who had a particular need. What makes the teaching experience so very rewarding is what the students, their parents, and even their siblings are getting out of it. When they come to thank me for what they have learned, sharing some of the things they learned and how they have grown, I get a knot in my throat and I get choked up. I become so keenly aware of God's presence in my life and in theirs, and I am so eternally grateful to God for what He did for ALL of us ... I am forever grateful that God has used me to help feed His spiritually-hungry flock!

20

One of the first things God has me teach groups on the journey of faith, beginning with the Christ Renews His Parish groups, is a special set of virtues with which He divinely inspired me. He now has me teach/share these virtues with ALL people with whom I interact, be it through ministry and evangelization efforts, with small groups, on retreats, in meetings, or through any other channel. Before God had *me* teach them, however, *He* taught them to *me*; God taught me to put them into practice and to model them, not just to speak them. These virtues, if lived fully, will encompass all the other many wonderful biblical virtues. They are **HUMILITY, FLEXIBILITY, OBEDIENCE, DISCIPLINE, ORDER, COMMITMENT**, and **LOVE.**

As I started to work with the Hispanic/Latino population that desired to experience a more profound and personal relationship with God, He started to do things in me. Clearly, God has changed me; He continues to allow me to change, and He causes me to grow. He did it first by humbling me. I am not an arrogant person, but I certainly have characteristics that God had to "tame" by refining me, molding me, and filling me ... so that He could use me ... for *His* purpose, as well as for His glory, praise, and honor.

A good generalization for people of my culture, the Hispanic/Latino culture, is that we are a humble, long-suffering people. I believe that more times than not, when someone has been long-suffering, has had to go with fewer resources, has not had the same opportunities as other people, and whose reliance has had to be on their faith and on God, that person is more apt to be humble. Culturally, we are taught to respect, to yield to another first, and to give before receiving; henceforth, **HUMILITY** generally tends to come a little easier for us, as a people.

Then God had to teach me **FLEXIBILITY**. I am a rather easy-going person, but regarding some things, I do know what I like and want and what I don't like and don't want. This makes me sometimes a little impatient with others, especially "repeat offenders," i.e., people who don't change from their ways that are offensive to or intrusive on others. By allowing myself to remain humble and then to be flexible, it is easier for me and for everyone else. I use scripture to help me be humble and flexible, as I use it for everything else in my life. In the book of Ecclesiastes, chapter 3, verses 1-8, we read that there is a time and a season for everything. I cannot begin to explain how this has helped me be more flexible, even when I don't want to be. I just have to remember that God is in control, so it is His plan, His time, and His purpose anyway.

The next virtue He gave me was **OBEDIENCE**. He had to teach me how to put it into practice in my own life before I could teach it to others. God wants us to be obedient to Him, to His Word, and to those in authority. Once again, it helps to remember that there is a time and a season and a purpose for everything under heaven. Some of us just don't like being told what to do. I've learned that I may not like what someone in authority is doing, how they are doing it, or how they exercise their authority, but I have options. The greatest option is to bring it to the Lord and to let Him guide me on how *He* wants me to handle any given situation. It makes it easier to practice obedience at times and in circumstances that go against our grain. The desire to obey God makes it easier to obey "man."

God then gave me the virtues of **DISCIPLINE** and **ORDER**. At times, the chronological order of these two virtues seems interchangeable, but they each hold their own. God taught me that I *must* have discipline in my life; there are things I should do and things I should not do. Activities, timeliness, behavior, and attitude – I need to be able to hold these in check and to control them, lest they control me. I must have the discipline to fight off temptation of any kind. When I subscribe to and apply the first three virtues, I have *discipline* in my life.

The Bible clearly tells us that God is a God of *order*. He shows us through both the Old and the New Testaments how order was essential to what was needed to be accomplished. God exemplified order when He led the Israelites out of Egypt and when He told Noah how to build the Ark, the Israelites how to build the new temple, the Jews how to bring their sacrificial offerings, and Abraham how to use the sacrificial ram He had substituted for his son, Isaac.

When there is order in my life, there is structure. Structure is not to be confused with inflexibility. I can be carefree and free-spirited, but without order, there is chaos. God is NOT a God of chaos. Chaos and clutter will distract and deter me from God and His purpose. It will take my mind off the things that are pure, that are true, and that are good. (Philippians 4:8-9) I will be too distracted to have order, and this of course, will make the enemy, i.e., Satan, happy. Applying these virtues into my daily life has made me a better, more credible person, especially among the people with whom I share them and to whom I teach them. Even in the face of trying and difficult circumstances, God has allowed me the grace to be a better, rather than a bitter, person. Consequently, I have learned to thank God for those trying and difficult times. I believe that each challenge I face is an opportunity to see God work powerfully on my behalf and an opportunity to share it with others.

The sixth virtue is **COMMITMENT**. We live in a world that does not want, or even know how, to commit. It wants to consider its options first. By waiting until the last minute to decide, we can get "the better option," "the best deal," or a "better choice." That is one thing that drives this world today. People either don't want, or are reticent, to commit. Consequently, we are at an all-time high of people living together outside of marriage – "to find out if we can handle living together," or "just in case it doesn't work out," or "in case we agree we don't want to be tied down," etc.

Sometimes people live together outside of marriage because they care for or love each other and because it is not hurting anyone and because they are going to get married anyway. At least that was what my husband and I convinced ourselves to believe, but now we regret having done it. We realize now that we were not living in God's will.

We regret what we did, we have repented, we have asked for forgiveness, and we know we have been forgiven. Praise God that He is a God of forgiveness and second chances. Since that realization, my husband and I have re-committed ourselves to one another, both in good times and in bad, in sickness and in health, and for as long as we both shall live.

The best part is that we have also committed ourselves to God; we are now a new creation. "Therefore, if anyone is in Christ, he is a new creation; the old has gone, the new has come!" (2 Corinthians 5:17) God has made us new, and we now enjoy a personal relationship with the Lord. When God finally got our attention, we found a love that is pure, solid, unconditional, steadfast, and perfect. We found it in our new relationship with God, AND, albeit not perfect, we found it in the newfound love we have for one another.

Lack of commitment exists all around us. People don't stay long at any one job. RSVPs to a special event arrive at the last minute, if at all. The risk here, which we tend to not consider, is the future. For example, what are we teaching our children? It is not commitment. What morals and values and character traits are we modeling to them? As mentioned previously, "Children learn what they live and live what they learn." What will

N.I.S.E.: The Transformation

our future look like when so many of our now younger people grow up learning the character traits that the world says are okay? What will our world look like when we cannot count on each other, when our word is no longer important and no longer our bond, when we will not commit to anything or to anyone? I can only thank God that His son, Jesus, committed to die for our sins so that we might live ... and that He then fulfilled that commitment.

The seventh and last virtue, to no big surprise, is **LOVE**. We can have these six other virtues, as well as *all* the other virtues in the world, that make for good, productive, healthy living, but if we have not love, we have nothing. God tells us that love is patient and love is kind. (1 Corinthians 13:4) Furthermore, we are told that we can do all kinds of good stuff, but if we don't have love, we are but a noisy gong. (1 Corinthians 13:1) I don't know about you, my friend, but I don't want to be a noisy gong.

21

God has revealed to me that in my old life, I had spent a long time being a noisy gong. Oh, I had love, but it was conditional. I did not realize it then, but I know it now. I am done with that. I don't want to be a noisy gong. I want others to feel love through me and to see love in me. Henceforth, I want others to be able to see God through my existence. However, whether or not others feel love *for* me is not my concern. While we might all want others to like or love us, it just is not going to happen all the time, especially as spiritual warfare comes into play. The world will hate us (those who choose to lead a Godly life), and the enemy will do its utmost to get others to hate us.

The worldly evils of jealously and lies and violence and murder and adultery and deceit, just to name a few – they are all like lions roaring, waiting to pounce and prey on the lamb. For that reason, I know that it is important to arm and clothe myself with the weapons God has given us to stand firm in the midst of spiritual warfare. God gives us the weapons of the *helmet of salvation,* the *breastplate of righteousness*, the *shield of faith,* the *belt of truth,* the *happy feet that carry the Good News,* the *two-edged sword* that is **God's Word,** and *the armor of prayer.* (Ephesians 6:10-18)

My own growth through these virtues has been not only spiritual but personal. I know that God has done a great work in me . . . for me . . . with me . . . because of me . . . and, mostly, in spite of me. He had to. If He is going to use me to share "necessary ingredients" for more Godly living with the world, then I must fully be the person God created and intended me to be. I know that I am a much, much better person since God first got my attention back when I thought I could barter with Him, when He showed me that He truly was real, and when He revealed His love for me . . . and ***I am so eternally grateful to God*** for ALL of it!!!

I think the biggest and most important thing that God has taught me in life, and that I believe He wants me to share with the rest of the world, is that He wants us to make ourselves **AVAILABLE** to Him, any time, all the time, and for all time. Once I learned this, I could do it. Once I did it, He indeed deepened His work in me, with me, through me, for me, and in spite of me. I believe that this is one of the purposes God has for *my* life – that I share and communicate this knowledge, insight, and wisdom with you and the rest of the world. I believe He gave me the necessary ingredients to do this in a simple way. I believe this was God's purpose for giving me the necessary ingredients for a simple existence, why He gave me NISE.

God knew the plans He had for me, plans to benefit me and prosper me, not to harm me, plans to give me hope and a future. (Jeremiah 29:11) I knew that He had prepared me for such a time as this. (Esther 4:14) I don't always understand it all; after all, His ways and His thoughts are far higher than mine are. (Isaiah 55:9) But as long as I remember to not be anxious about ANYTHING, but in ALL things, through prayer, petition and thanksgiving, bring all things before the Lord, then a peace, God's peace, that transcends all understanding shall be given unto me, and my heart and my mind shall be protected in Christ Jesus. (Philippians 4:4-7) I know that all things happen in God's time, not mine, for His timing is perfect. I make mistakes, but God does not!

Such are the promises of God – the beautiful promises, found in both the Old Testament and the New Testament. Some promises we are very familiar with, others we may not recognize, but we trust and believe that God's Word is faithful, and it is sovereign. We trust what God tells us – that His Word will not come back void. (Isaiah 55:11) Praise God for that!

Through the years, since I gave my life to the Lord, I have been used in ways that I cannot begin to explain other than, as I mentioned earlier, "God does not call the equipped, but He equips the called." That certainly is what He did with me. We know that "**there is no co-incidence, only God-incidence**." God knows very well what He is going to do with whom and how He is going to use them. After all, He knew us even before we were in the womb. (Jeremiah 1:5) He taught me so many things that He has allowed me to share with others; I know that we are *all* better people because of those teachings.

I feel that I am just the most blessed person in the whole wide world! And I will thank the Lord until my dying day for every experience He has given me and allowed me to have that is molding and shaping me into being the woman God created me to be.

And so . . . He has me here writing this NISE book for you to read, and this is just the beginning. There is so much more. God has so much more for me, for you, for anyone **AND** for everyone who will avail themselves to Him, to His voice, and to His Word. It is that simple. God wants us to make ourselves available to Him. He wants us to know how much He loves us. He wants us to love Him with all our heart, with all our soul, with all our strength, and with all our mind. (Deuteronomy 6:5, 10:12, Mark 12:30, and Luke 10:27) Then He wants us to love our neighbor as ourselves. (Mark 12:31, Luke 10:27) Once we do, He can do amazing and truly awesome things with and through us.

I know that God's plan is to reach others with these NISE little books ... books of stories of encouragement, of inspiration, of immense love and passion, of anecdotes, of pearls of wisdom, of simple living, of experiencing God in extraordinary ways through our ordinary living, of acknowledging God in our life, etc. I don't think we can ever have too much 'NISE' or nice in our lives, nor can we ever finish being 'NISE' or nice.

This is just the beginning. This is God's work. Just as God is endless and infinite ... for He has no beginning and no end, and He is the alpha and the omega (Revelation 1:8) ... so are the possibilities of possessing necessary ingredients for a simple existence. The key here is nice and "simple." God wants us to live simply, that we may simply live. Imagine if we all chose to live life that way – wouldn't that be nice?

ACKNOWLEDGEMENTS

We've heard the saying that "No man is an island." This is something I want to clearly acknowledge up front. I would be remiss if I did not acknowledge that while I am the one who physically wrote this book, I did so with divine intervention. I give God all the glory for this book and for all the NISE books that are yet to come. At one time in my life, I would have said that the writing of these books is long overdue. However, I recognize that the time is perfect because it is God's time and not mine. Without God in my life, there would be no NISE books to be written. Thank you, God.

This book was made possible through the love, encouragement, and support of my family; I am forever grateful to them. My husband, Jack, has made it possible for me to do all that I do and to be all that I am in life. His belief and faith in me helped me to have faith and belief in myself. While he is not a perfect husband, he's pretty close, and he *is* the perfect husband for me! Doing the things in life that allowed me to have the experiences that I did, which in turn enabled me to write this book, was possible because of his patience, understanding, encouragement, support, and willingness to fend for himself on the home front, as well as to carry my load along with his. His willingness to assume the majority of the responsibilities at home made it possible for me to serve God by serving others. My life journey and mission have taken me away from my home life and my family more than I care to remember, particularly since we have become "empty nesters." Through it all, my family, and in particular, my husband, has patiently persevered. Thank you, Jack.

My daughters have been my biggest cheerleaders. They have gifted me with so much, and the greatest gift of all has been their unconditional love. They know that I have wanted to write these books ever since they were little girls. I would share with them that I knew God was calling me to write books. I know that they are truly happy for me that I am realizing not just my dream, but my life's mission and calling. My attorney daughter, Jacqueline, has helped me by taking care of things that I have needed for the publication of this book, and by invaluably identifying grammatical errors that snuck past our family's keen editing eyes. My youngest daughter, Veronica, a former resident of California and now a resident of Arizona, has read and re-read the book for me, helping me through to the end. They each did so much, using their own strengths and talents, to help this book become a reality. Without them and Jack, this book would not be what it is. Thank you, Jacqueline and Veronica.

I would also like to acknowledge my good and longtime friend, Karyl Rickard. She encouraged me when I did not realize I needed encouragement. She believed in me when I did not believe in myself. She pushed me. And she loved me through it all. Because of her, I attended a writer's conference that allowed me to write this book in its initial stage in one weekend. Thank you, Karyl.

I want to acknowledge my colleague and friend, Lydia, for her initial help in getting this book translated into Spanish. Thank you, Lydia. My utmost personal goal is that this book gets into the hands of all Spanish speakers whom I personally know, as well as all others who might benefit from it.

I would also be remiss if I did not thank ALL my friends and family for their words of encouragement, and especially for their prayers. I thank all who kept asking me about my book and who encouraged me in any number of ways. Saying that they wanted to buy my book without even seeing it or reading any of it was the greatest compliment they could have given me.

In addition, I want to acknowledge that I could not have begun to publish this book had it not been for Jack, Henry, Robyn, Vince, Karyl and Gene, all of whom showed their faith in me through their investment in this book. I will be forever grateful for their encouragement in such a tangible way. Jack, Henry, Robyn, Vince, Karyl, and Gene – my sincerest and deepest gratitude to each one of you.

And finally, I want to acknowledge God, through whom all good things come and all things are possible. In chapter four, verse 13 of Philippians it says, "I can do all things through Christ who strengthens me." Indeed, He just proved to me the truth of His Word. Thank You, my Lord and my God. Thank you for this NISE book.

www.ingramcontent.com/pod-product-compliance
Lightning Source LLC
Chambersburg PA
CBHW031646040426
42453CB00006B/226